Sue Kay, Vaughan Jones

American Inside Out

Ana. ♥

Student's Book

B

Pre-intermediate

MACMILLAN

Macmillan Education
Between Towns Road, Oxford OX4 3PP
A division of Macmillan Publishers Limited
Companies and representatives throughout the world

ISBN 978 1 4050 2454 9

Text © Sue Kay, Vaughan Jones and Philip Kerr 2002
Design and illustration © Macmillan Publishers Limited 2002

First published 2002
American Edition 2004

Project management by Desmond O'Sullivan, ELT Publishing
Services.
Designed by Jackie Hill, 320 Design.
Illustrated by Martin Chatterton pp. 127, 128; Rebecca Halls pp. 77,
122, 123; Ed McLachlan pp. 88, 92, 116; Julian Mosedale pp. 91, 121;
Mark Thomas p. 117.
Cover design by Andrew Oliver.
Cover painting *After Visiting David Hockney* © Howard Hodgkin.

Authors' acknowledgments
We would like to thank all our colleagues at the Lake School, Oxford,
for their help and continued support; in particular, Pete Maggs, whose
thoughtful comments on work in progress were much appreciated.
Thanks also go to our pre-intermediate students who have kept us
focused at all times on what works in the classroom (and made sure
that we disregarded everything else).
We are especially grateful to Helena Gomm and John Hird for the
Inside Out Teacher's Book, to Pete Maggs for the weekly *Inside Out*
e-lessons, to Guy Jackson for running the *Inside Out* Web site at
www.insideout.net, which has finally come of age, and to everybody
involved in the *Inside Out* Resource Pack: a great team!
At Macmillan Education we would like to thank Sue Bale (publishing
director), David Riley (publisher), and Pippa McNee (picture researcher).
We would also like to thank Alyson Maskell and Celia Bingham
(freelance editors), Jackie Hill (freelance designer), Helen Reilly
(freelance picture researcher), Paulette McKean (freelance permissions
editor), as well as James Richardson and Vince Cross (freelance
audio producers). Thanks also go to the production and marketing
teams who have worked so hard to make *Inside Out* what it is.
Once again, we reserve the biggest thank you of all for Desmond
O'Sullivan (freelance project manager). We are indeed privileged to
be working with such a talented and committed professional—
long may it continue! Thanks for everything, Des.
In addition, we must thank our families, without whose support
and understanding none of this would have been possible.
We would also like to thank Thalia Carr (The Swan School, Oxford),
Jenny Johnson (International House, Barcelona), Beth Neher
(International House, London), and Katarzyna Kowalczyk
(Macmillan Polska) for their very helpful comments.

The authors and publishers would like to thank the following for
permission to reproduce their material:
Don't Worry, Be Happy. Words and music by Bobby McFerrin © Prob
Noblem Music/BMG Music Publishing Ltd., Bedford House, 69–79
Fulham High Street, London, SW6 1994, reprinted by permission of
Music Sales Limited. All rights reserved. International Copyright Secured.
Excerpt from *Billy Elliot* by Melvin Burgess. Screenplay by Lee Hall
(The Chicken House, 2001), text copyright © Melvin Burgess 2001.
Original screenplay by Lee Hall © Universal Studios Publishing Rights,
a division of Universal Studios Licensing Inc., 2001, reprinted by
permission of the publisher. All rights reserved. Excerpt from "Why I
Bought My Child A Gun" by Phil Hogan, copyright © the *Guardian*
2001, from the *Guardian* 07.04.01, reprinted by permission of the
author. Excerpt from "104 Things to Do with a Banana" by Wayne
M. Hilburn from www.dmgi.com/bananas.html, reprinted by
permission of the author. Excerpt from "Balloon Buddies," the
Daily Mail 06.28.01, reprinted by permission of Atlantic Syndication
Partners. Excerpt from "Slip Sliding Away" by Sophie Radice,
copyright © Sophie Radice 2001, from the *Guardian Weekend*
11.03.01, reprinted by permission of the author. Excerpt from *The
Lost Continent* by Bill Bryson (Blackswan, a division of Transworld
Publishers, 1999), copyright © Bill Bryson 1989, reprinted by
permission of the publisher. *24 Hours from Tulsa*. Words by Hal
David. Music by Burt Bacharach. © Hidden Valley Music Company/
Casa David, USA. Universal/MCA Music Limited, Elsinore House,
77 Fulham Palace Road, London W6 8JA (50%), Windswept Pacific
Music (London) Limited, Hope House, 40 St. Peter's Road, London
W6 9BD (50%), reprinted by permission of Windswept Music
(London) Ltd. and Music Sales Ltd. All rights reserved. International
Copyright Secured.

The authors and publishers wish to thank the following for
permission to reproduce their photographs:
Ardea pp. 102, 105 (t); Art Explosion p.112 (t); David Bebber p. 108
(tr); Jenny Cockell p. 109; Corbis pp. 73 (bl), 112 (m); Paul Cousans
p. 108 (tl); Fortean pp. 100, 106, 107; Getty Images pp. 64 (a–c), 65
(all), 69, 71 (all), 78 (all), 82 (both), 83, 85, 95, 99, 100, 101, 102 (a,
b, c, d, f), 103 (all), 108 (mr, bl), 110 (both), 114, 119, B124, B126
(m, r); Greg Evans Picture Library p. 112 (b); Alberto Korda
Guerillero Heroico (Che Guevara) © ADAGP Paris and DACS London
2002 courtesy of Couturier Gallery LA p. 74; Magnum p. 94;
Desmond O'Sullivan p. 104; Photodisc p. 99; Popperfoto p. 70;
Powerstock pp. 64 (t), 75; Retna pp. 67, 73 (br); Rex Features Ltd.
pp. 73 (l), 77, 86, 117, 118, B126 (l); Science Photo Library p. 111;
Louis Stettner *Promenade Brooklyn 1954* © ADAGP Paris and DACS
London 2002 courtesy of Gallery 292 / Howard Greenberg Gallery p.
68.

Commissioned photographs by Haddon Davies p. 97 (food images).
The publishers wish to thank Lou Wright.

Cartoons on p. 85 reproduced with permission from Tony Husband;
p. 84 with permission from *Private Eye*; p. 61 with permission from
The Spectator; pp. 79, 113 with permission from Cartoonstock;
p. 86 with permission from *Business Life*; p. 72 with permission from
Punch.

Printed and bound in Thailand

2013 2012 2011 2010 2009
12   11   10   9   8

11 Smile

Work in small groups. Look at this expression and discuss the questions.

Say "cheese"!

- When do people say this?
- What do you say in your language?
- Do you find it easy to smile in photographs?

Vocabulary: the face

1 Use words from the photograph below to complete the following article about smiling. Choose an appropriate singular or plural form for each word.

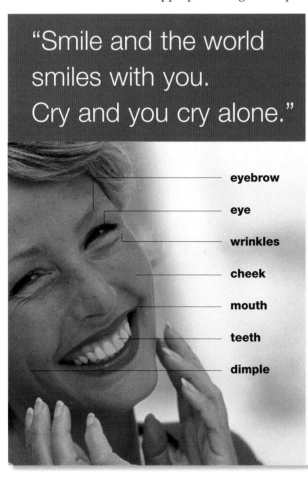

"Smile and the world smiles with you. Cry and you cry alone."

- eyebrow
- eye
- wrinkles
- cheek
- mouth
- teeth
- dimple

According to research from the United States, we smile for many different reasons.

- There's the listener/response smile. When two people are having a conversation, the listener smiles to encourage the speaker.
- There's the polite smile. This is the kind of smile you make when your aunt gives you a horrible birthday present.
- There's the miserable smile—for example, when you go to the dentist and he tells you that you need to have a (1) ____ taken out.

Very often, these social smiles are not real; they are "fake" smiles. Fake smiles are easy to do—you just have to tighten the muscles on your (2) ____ .

But there's only one smile that is the smile of true enjoyment. This smile is extremely hard to fake. It involves the muscles at the corners of the (3) ____ and the muscles around the eyes.

When someone gives a true smile, the (4) ____ get smaller, and you see little (5) ____ around the edge. The (6) ____ go up, and on some people, (7) ____ appear in their cheeks.

The genuine smile of enjoyment not only makes us feel good, but makes others feel good too.

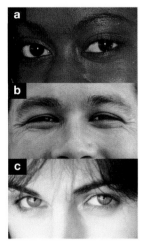

2 [cassette] **46** Listen and check your answers. How many different smiles are mentioned? Can you do all these smiles? Show your partner.

3 Look at the photo in 1 again and check (✓) the features you can see.

> bags under the eyes   beard   beautiful teeth   false eyelashes   freckles
> mustache   pale skin   wavy hair

4 Which of these features do you like on a man or a woman? Describe your ideal face to your partner.

5 Work with a partner. Look at the pairs of eyes on the left. According to the text, which ones do you think are smiling? How can you tell? Look at page B124 to see the complete faces. Which ones did you guess correctly?

/s/, /z/, or /ɪz/? **1** 🔊 **47** Listen and repeat these nouns. In each set, underline the noun where the final "s" is pronounced differently from the others.

a) ears eyes cheeks legs
b) lips hands toes arms
c) dimples freckles wrinkles eyelashes

2 Put the nouns from the box into the appropriate columns, depending on the sound of the final "s." Add the nouns from 1. The first ones have been done for you.

backs knees noses chins mustaches wrists heads shoulders stomachs beards	+ /s/	+ /z/	+ /ɪz/
	backs	knees	noses

3 🔊 **48** Listen, repeat the words, and check your answers. Which of the nouns in 2 would you not expect to use in the plural when describing someone?

Vocabulary: describing character **1** The way you smile can show what kind of person you are. Read the article below and match one of the headings (a–d) to each paragraph (1–4).

a) Shy and sensitive   b) Sassy and impertinent   c) Confident   d) Sociable

What's in a Smile?

1 This is the smile of a joker. The raised eyebrows and dimples in the cheeks show a good sense of humor and a warm personality. This person is often a rebel—with little respect for authority.

2 The wide, toothy smile shows that people like this are easygoing and friendly. They enjoy being in a crowd and are a lot of fun to go out with. They're always looking for the next party.

3 The smile is in the eyes. This is a sensitive person and a loyal friend. This kind of person thinks before speaking, is a good listener, and doesn't like to be the center of attention in a crowd.

4 This is a smile that says, "I know it all." These people are very sure of themselves. They like a good argument, and they usually win. They're hard-working and very ambitious. And they can be very bossy.

2 🔊 **49** Listen and check your answers.

3 🔊 **50** Listen to six different people talking and use the most appropriate adjective in the box to describe each one.

ambitious bossy confident sensitive sociable easygoing

LANGUAGE TOOLBOX

affectionate cold dark
deep frightening
independent loyal
mysterious nasty
selfish stormy strong
sweet unpleasant

4 Use any of the adjectives in the Language Toolbox or your own ideas to take this personality test.

Write one word to describe each of the following.

• a dog _____   • a cat _____   • a rat _____   • coffee _____   • an ocean _____

5 Turn to page B124 to find out the meaning of what you have written. Do you think it's accurate? Tell your partner.

What Are You Like?

Reading   **1**   Answer the questionnaire below. For each situation, choose *a, b,* or *c,* according to what you are most likely to say. Then calculate your score, read what it means on page B124, and compare with a partner.

Optimist or Pessimist –
What Are You?

1   **It's Sunday, and you're in the middle of a long walk in the country. It starts to rain.**
   a   It always rains when I go for a walk.
   b   It could be worse—it could be snowing.
   c   Great! I really enjoy walking in the rain.

2   **You arrive home after a great vacation.**
   a   I don't want to go back to work.
   b   I'm going to start planning my next vacation. I want to have something to look forward to.
   c   The vacation was great, but now I'm looking forward to sleeping in my own bed.

3   **It's your 40th birthday.**
   a   The best years of my life are over.
   b   I'm getting older—so what? It happens to everybody.
   c   I hope to live to 100—where's the party?!

4   **You have a cold.**
   a   I need to see a doctor as soon a possible.
   b   I need to buy some tissues.
   c   It's just a cold—it won't kill me.

5   **Your partner has ended your relationship.**
   a   I've had enough of men/women. I'm never going to fall in love again.
   b   I know I'll get over it, but it might take a long time.
   c   He/She wasn't the right one for me.

6   **You have to make an important life decision.**
   a   Whatever I decide to do, it will be the wrong decision.
   b   I'm going to take my time and think carefully about my decision.
   c   Whatever I decide to do, it will be the right decision.

7   **It's autumn.**
   a   I don't like autumn because it will soon be winter.
   b   It's just another time of year.
   c   It's a beautiful time of year.

8   **You unexpectedly inherit $5,000.**
   a $5,000 isn't going to change my life.
   b   Great! I can buy a few luxuries that I couldn't afford before.
   c   This must be my lucky day—I think I'll buy a lottery ticket.

How to score   Each time you answer **a**, score 1.   Each time you answer **b**, score 2.   Each time you answer **c**, score 3.

2   Who got the highest and lowest score in the class?

Vocabulary: **1**   Complete these statements by choosing the appropriate structure. Refer to examples in
verb patterns   the questionnaire if necessary.

   a)   I want **to be**/**being** extremely rich.
   b)   I'm looking forward to **go out**/**going out** tonight.
   c)   I've decided **to get up**/**getting up** early even on the weekend.
   d)   I enjoy **to speak**/**speaking** English.
   e)   I need **to spend**/**spending** more time at home.
   f)   I hope **to go**/**going** on a great vacation next summer.

2   Do you think any of the sentences are true for your partner? Ask questions to find out.

3   Use the same verb structures to write six more sentences that are true for you. Compare them with a partner.

   For example: *I don't want to get married until I'm thirty.*
              I'm looking forward to finishing my education.

Don't Worry, Be Happy

Song

1 Make word pairs by matching a word from list A with a word from list B that rhymes.

A	B
style	bed
trouble	smile
head	note
frown	double
late	down
wrote	litigate

2 [cassette] **51** You are going to listen to a song called *Don't Worry, Be Happy*. Read the song and complete each verse with the word pairs from 1. Then listen and check your answers.

3 Find at least three reasons for worrying that are mentioned in the song.

4 Work with a partner. Discuss what you think the biggest worries are for the following people.

a) a child
b) a 14-year-old girl
c) a 16-year-old boy
d) a college student
e) a parent
f) a grandparent

How does this song make *you* feel? What music makes you feel happy? Tell your partner.

Don't Worry, Be Happy

A huge hit in 1988 for singer, composer, and conductor Bobby McFerrin.

Here's a little song I (1) _____ .
You might want to sing it note for (2) _____ .
Don't worry, be happy.

In every life we have some (3) _____ .
When you worry you make it (4) _____ .
Don't worry, be happy.

Ain't got no place to lay your (5) _____ ?
Somebody came and took your (6) _____ ?
Don't worry, be happy.

The landlord says your rent is (7) _____ ?
He may have to (8) _____ .
Don't worry, be happy.

Ain't got no cash, ain't got no (9) _____ ?
Ain't got no girl to make you (10) _____ ?
Don't worry, be happy.

'Cos when you worry, your
face will (11) _____ .
That will bring everybody
(12) _____ .
Don't worry, be happy.

Close-up

Imperatives

1 Choose a correct alternative way of saying "Be happy" from the following.

a) Be not sad.   b) Don't sad you.   c) Don't be sad.   d) Don't you sad.

2 Look at the following imperatives. Give an alternative way of saying the same thing by using the adjectives in parentheses.

a) Be good. (naughty) *Don't be naughty.*
b) Be quiet! (noisy)   e) Behave yourself. (rude)   h) Calm down. (angry)
c) Be on time. (late)   f) Cheer up. (miserable)   i) Act your age. (childish)
d) Be nice. (mean)   g) Say what you think. (shy)

3 Work with a partner. Choose an imperative from 2 and write a three-line dialogue to show a typical situation where it could be used.

For example: A: *I'll see you at 8:30 outside the theater.*
                      B: *Don't be late!*
                      A: *Don't worry. I'm never late.*

Language Reference: Imperatives

We use an imperative form when we are telling somebody to do something or not to do something: orders, advice, encouragement, etc.
Come here.   Be quiet!   Don't be shy.   Come on.   Hurry up!

Take It Easy

1 Imagine that today is "No-Stress Day."
Read the article on the right and answer
the questions. Discuss your answers with a
partner.

a) Which suggestion is the easiest for
you to do?
b) Which suggestion is the most difficult
for you to do?
c) Which is the best or worst suggestion?

2 Work with a partner. Add three of your
own suggestions to the list.

**Vocabulary:
phrasal verbs**

1 Complete the sentences using these
phrasal verbs from the article.

> give up   hang up   put on
> turn off   turn on   take off
> throw away

a) I always *take off* my shoes before I go
into my house.
b) If I want to relax, I _turn off_ all the lights
and sit in silence.
c) When I want to look my best, I _put on_
a suit.
d) I could never _give up_ smoking—it's the
only thing that helps me relax.
e) The first thing I do when I get to the
office is _turn on_ my computer.
f) I never _throw away_ plastic bags, because
they're so useful.
g) I never do any ironing. I just _hang up_ my
clothes very carefully when they come
out of the washing machine.

2 Are any of the sentences true for you?
Discuss with a partner.

16 Ways to De-stress

1 Take off your watch.

2 Turn off your cell phone.

3 Don't eat your breakfast on
your feet—sit down and enjoy it.

4 Put on your most comfortable
clothes.

5 Don't run after the bus—let it go.

6 Smell the roses.

7 Give up the gym.

8 Fall in love.

9 Turn on your television only if
there's something you really want
to watch.

10 Throw away any clothes you haven't
worn in the past two years.

11 Laugh.

12 Hang up your clothes when you
take them off.

13 Spend ten minutes doing absolutely
nothing.

14 Walk.

15 Do the ironing only if you love it.

16 Put on your favorite
music and turn
up the volume.

Close-up

Phrasal verbs

1 Work with a partner. Look at the three phrasal verbs used in these sentences and answer the questions.

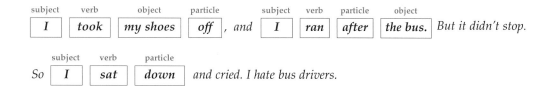

subject	verb	object	particle		subject	verb	particle	object	
I	took	my shoes	off	, and	I	ran	after	the bus.	But it didn't stop.

	subject	verb	particle	
So	I	sat	down	and cried. I hate bus drivers.

a) Which phrasal verb does not take an object?
b) Which phrasal verb can have the object between the verb and the particle? (SEPARABLE)
c) Which phrasal verb always has the object after the particle? (NONSEPARABLE)

2 When the object is a pronoun such as *it, them,* or *her,* where do you always put it when the phrasal verb is: a) separable? b) nonseparable?

3 Put the words in the right order to make answers to the questions. Look the phrasal verbs up in a dictionary if you are not sure.

a) What should I do with this banana skin? (away throw it) *Throw it away.*
b) What should I do with this mess? (it up clean) *clean it up*
c) What should I do about this problem? (it deal with) *deal with it*
d) What should I do with this application form? (fill out it) *Fill it out*
e) What should I do with my grandmother's wedding ring? (away it put) *put it away*
f) What should I do about my party? Nobody can come. (it call off) *Call it off*

Language Reference: Phrasal verbs

The term "phrasal verb" usually refers to all multi-word verbs consisting of a verb + particle(s). Phrasal verbs can be divided into three basic types.

1 verb + particle
Some phrasal verbs are intransitive and so do not take a direct object.
Sit down and enjoy it. When are you going to ***grow up***?

2 verb + object + particle (SEPARABLE)
The biggest group of phrasal verbs are transitive. When the direct object is a noun, we can put it before or after the particle.
Take off your shoes. ***Take*** your shoes ***off***.
When the direct object is a pronoun, we must put it between the verb and the particle.
Turn it ***off***, please. NOT ~~Turn off it~~

3 verb + particle + object (NONSEPARABLE)
With this type of phrasal verb, we always put the direct object—noun or pronoun—after the particle.
She ***takes after*** her grandmother. I ***ran after*** it, but the bus didn't stop.

Laughter—the Best Medicine

1 🔲 52 Listen to a report about laughter—without laughing. What are the benefits of laughter?

2 Work with a partner. Sit facing each other. Student A: Try to make student B smile and/or laugh by saying funny things. Student B: Try to keep a straight face. Take turns making each other smile and/or laugh.

12 Rebel

May Day

Reading

1 Work with a partner. Look at the photograph below and discuss the following questions.

    a) What do you think is happening?
    b) What things do people demonstrate about in your country?
    c) Have you ever seen or taken part in a demonstration? What was it about?

2 Read the article. Are the following statements true or false?

    a) Many of the protesters disagree with globalization. T
    b) Twelve protesters were arrested in Sydney, Australia. F
    c) Demonstrations in Winnipeg were peaceful. T
    d) In Norway, a protester threw a bottle at the foreign minister. F
    e) Three hundred demonstrators were arrested in Portland, Oregon. F

3 Do you think demonstrations are a good way of making a point?

Global May Day Protest

Around the world, thousands of people took part in protest marches and demonstrations today.
5 Many of the protesters were demonstrating against globalization. Demonstrations were peaceful in most places, but in Sydney, Australia,
10 violence broke out, and dozens of protesters were arrested.
    Police in Winnipeg, Canada, prepared for violence, but the demonstration was more like a
15 big street party than a protest.
    In Norway, a protester threw an apple pie in the face of foreign minister Thorbjoern Jagland.
20   In Portland, Oregon, peaceful demonstrators gathered downtown. When the police told them to leave, the protesters became violent and police fired
25 rubber bullets at 300 marchers. Sixteen people were arrested.

What are You Doing Here?

Listening

1 At May Day demonstrations around the world, not everybody demonstrates against the same thing. Match the slogans (*a–e*) with the causes (*1–5*).

a) NO TO MULTINATIONALS   1 Against nuclear weapons

b) SAVE THE TREES   2 Against cruelty to animals

c) STOP STAR WARS   3 Against globalization

d) BAN ANIMAL TESTING   4 Against destruction of the environment

e) EQUAL PAY FOR EQUAL WORK   5 Against unequal pay for women

2 🔊 **53** You are going to listen to radio interviews with the four protesters in the photos on the right. Before you listen, look at the photos and try to match the people with the slogans and causes in 1. Listen and check your answers.

3

Jake, 23, college student

5

sto p!!

Debbie, 27, housewife

2

Ronny, 27, cook

4

Caroline, 23, teacher

Vocabulary: protest

1 Complete the sentences below, using these words from the recordings in the previous section.

> against   anti-   supporter of   don't feel
> in favor   really care   support

a) I'm a _supporter of_ peaceful action.

b) I'm _in favor_ of many of the causes here.

c) I'm not _anti_ men—I just want a fairer system.

d) I'm _against_ animal testing.

e) I _support_ animal rights.

f) I _don't feel_ strongly about politics.

g) I _really care_ about a clean, safe environment for our children.

2 Work with a partner. Discuss the statements in 1. Which ones are true for you?

3 What causes do you feel most strongly about? Compare with a partner.

Vocabulary: word families

1 What are the noun forms for the following verbs: *pollute, globalize, demonstrate, inform*?

For example: *pollute – pollution*

2 🔊 **54** Add each verb and noun pair from 1 to the chart according to their stress pattern. Listen, repeat, and check your answers.

A		B		C		D	
Verb	Noun	Verb	Noun	Verb	Noun	Verb	Noun
▪■	▪■▪	▪■	▪▪■▪	■▪▪	▪▪■▪	■▪▪	▪▪▪■▪
pollute	pollution	____	____	____	____	____	____

3 🔊 **55** Listen and repeat eight more verb/noun pairs. Add them to the appropriate columns in the chart in 2. On which syllable does the stress fall when a noun ends in *-ion*?

Close-up

Dad, you're shaving with my cell phone.

Dynamic and stative meanings

1 Work with a partner. Look at the verbs in these three excerpts from the radio interviews in the previous section. Discuss the questions.

"People are handing out leaflets with information."
"We're demonstrating for equal pay."
"I'm having fun with my friends."

a) Do the verbs describe actions or states? *actions*
b) What is the name of the tense used in all three excerpts? *Present continuous*

2 Rewrite these sentences by putting the verb in parentheses in the present continuous tense.

a) A phone (ring). *A phone is ringing.*
b) A teacher in another class (talk).
c) The traffic (make) a lot of noise.
d) A clock (tick).
e) A student (laugh).
f) People (chat).

3 Work as a class. Listen in silence for fifteen seconds and check (✓) the actions in 2 that are true. Write down other things that are happening.

4 Work with a partner. Look at the verbs in three more excerpts from the radio interviews in the previous section. Discuss the questions.

"I just want a fairer system."
"I have three dogs, two cats, and a pet mouse."
"I don't know much about it."

a) Do the verbs describe *actions* or *states*?
b) What is the name of the tense used in all three excerpts?
c) Is it possible to use a continuous tense with verbs when they describe a state?

5 From the excerpts in 1 and 4, which verb has two different meanings and describes both an action and a state?

6 Work with a partner. Decide if the verbs in parentheses describe an action or a state. Put the verb into an appropriate form to complete the sentences.

a) Jane (like) James Bond movies. *likes*
b) Tony (know) how to play the piano. *knows*
c) Marta (have) a television in her bedroom. *has*
d) Julie (have) difficulty with this exercise. *is having*
e) Brian (look) like his father. *looks*
f) Ryan (look) for a new place to live. *is looking*
g) Sue (think) of going out tonight. *is thinking*
h) Rosa (think) war is stupid. *thinks*

7 Replace the names in 6 with names of students in the class to make as many true sentences as you can. Ask questions to help you.

For example: *Do you like James Bond movies?   Are you thinking of going out tonight?*

Language Reference: Dynamic and stative meanings

Dynamic meanings: actions

Most verbs have dynamic meanings. They describe actions: Something "happens." We can use them with continuous forms to talk about activities in progress.

*People **are chatting**.*

Stative meanings: states

Some verbs connected with knowledge, emotion, or possession have stative meanings. They describe states: Nothing "happens." We cannot use them with continuous forms.

*I **don't feel** strongly about politics.*

Note: Some verbs such as *have*, *look*, and *think* can have both dynamic and stative meanings.

*Rosie **is looking** for a new place to live. (look = dynamic meaning)*
*Brian **looks** like his father. (look = stative meaning)*

Celebrity Rebels

Reading   **1**   You are going to read an article about three famous people who have all rebelled against their family in different ways. Read the article and find out who...

a) <u>joined</u> a political group. *Patty H*
b) <u>committed a crime</u>. *Patricia*
c) <u>began</u> smoking as a teenager. *Macaulay c*
d) <u>colored</u> his/her hair. *Macaulay culkin*
e) had <u>inappropriate</u> relationships. *P SM*
f) <u>left home to live with</u> the circus. *PSM*

REBEL REBEL

Patty Hearst

On February 4, 1974, Patricia Hearst, the 19-year-old daughter of a very wealthy businessman, was kidnapped by a revolutionary political group called the Symbionese Liberation Army (SLA).

She was held prisoner for 57 days while the kidnappers waited for her parents to pay the ransom.

But they didn't pay the ransom, and so Patty decided to rebel against her family. She became a member of the SLA and was renamed Tania.

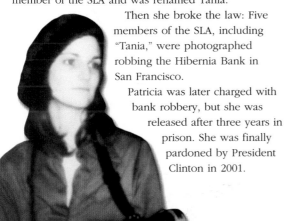

Then she broke the law: Five members of the SLA, including "Tania," were photographed robbing the Hibernia Bank in San Francisco.

Patricia was later charged with bank robbery, but she was released after three years in prison. She was finally pardoned by President Clinton in 2001.

Princess Stephanie of Monaco

Princess Stephanie is the younger daughter of Prince Rainier of Monaco. She is known as the "rebel royal," mainly because of her unsuitable relationships. She married one of her bodyguards and had two children. She then divorced him and had a relationship (and a third child) with another bodyguard.

After that she was photographed in a circus caravan with Franco Knie, an elephant trainer—in other words, the rebel royal ran away with the circus!

Macaulay Culkin

Macaulay Culkin was born on August 26, 1980, in New York, the third of seven children. "Mack," as his friends call him, starred in the movie *Home Alone*, which made him one of the most famous and richest child stars of all time.

In 1995, his parents separated and started fighting over Mack's money. Disgusted with his parents' behavior, Mack refused to accept any movie roles until they stopped fighting.

Then, at the age of 17, he started smoking, dyed his hair pink, and got married.

2   Replace the <u>underlined</u> words in 1 with words or expressions from the text.

3   Work with a partner. Discuss the following questions.

- Who do you think is the most rebellious of the three people?
- In what other ways do people rebel against their families?
- In what ways did you rebel against your family when you were younger?

Anecdote   Think about a time when you got into trouble as a child. You are going to tell your partner about it. Choose from the list the things you want to talk about. Think about what you will say and the language you will need.

☐ How old were you?
☐ Where were you?
☐ Were you alone or with other people?
☐ What did you do?
☐ Why did you do it?

☐ Did you know it was wrong?
☐ What did you feel like afterward?
☐ Who caught you?
☐ What happened to you?
☐ Did you ever do the same thing again?

Close-up

Language Reference p. 75

Passives

1 Work with a partner. Look at the question and two alternative answers (*1* and *2*) below. Discuss why the second answer is the more natural alternative. Then choose the correct explanation (*a* or *b*).

What happened to
Patty Hearst on
February 4, 1974?

1

subject	verb	object
A revolutionary political group	kidnapped	her.

2

subject	verb	*by*	agent
She	was kidnapped	by	a revolutionary political group.

a)   Because the question is about Patty Hearst. We usually start sentences with the person or thing that we are interested in.

b)   Because Patty Hearst was a very rich and important woman.

2 Work with a partner. Refer to answers *1* and *2* in the last exercise. Discuss the following.

a)   Which tense are both answers in?

b)   In which answer is the verb in the passive form?

c)   Which auxiliary verb combines with a past participle to form the passive?

3 Here are the main events from the Patty Hearst story. Complete the following task.

a)   Put each verb in the most appropriate form: active or passive.

b)   Put the events in the correct order and retell the story.

c)   Check your answers in the text on page 73.

( ) a) She (**charge**) with bank robbery. *was charged*

( ) b) She (**rename**) "Tania." *was renamed*

( ) c) She (**hold**) prisoner for 57 days. *was held*

( ) d) She (**photograph**) robbing a bank. *photographed*

( ) e) She (**decide**) to rebel against her family. *decide*

( ) f) She (**pardon**) by President Clinton in 2001. *was pardoned*

( ) g) She (**release**) after three years in prison. *was released*

( ) h) She (**become**) a member of the SLA. *became*

(1) i) She (**kidnap**) by a revolutionary political group. *was kidnapped* *kidnapped*

( ) j) She (**break**) the law. *broke*

4 Use simple past passives to complete the article about Che Guevara.

IMAGE OF A REBEL

IT is an image that became a legend of the twentieth century. It is tattooed on Diego Maradona's arm. A Che poster (1 **pin**) ***was pinned*** on Mick Jagger's wall when he was a student, and millions of T-shirts are still decorated with the image today. The picture (2 **take**) *was* on March 5, 1960, at a memorial service in Havana, Cuba. Cuban photographer Alberto Korda (3 **send**) *was sent* by the magazine *Revolución* to take photographs of the Cuban leader Fidel Castro.

"Che was standing behind Fidel Castro on the platform," said Korda. "You couldn't see him. Then suddenly he stepped forward to the edge of the platform. I managed to take a photo. Then he was gone."

Seven years later, in October 1967, Che Guevara (4 **kill**) *was* in Bolivia, and Korda's photograph became an icon for revolutionaries everywhere. Korda's photographs (5 **exhibit**) *were exhibited* in Paris in Spring 2001. It was while he was attending the exhibition of his work that Korda died.

5 🖭 **56** Listen and check your answers.

6 Think of famous people that you admire. Whose picture would you like to have…

a) on a poster on your wall?   b) on your T-shirt?   c) tattooed on your arm?

Language Reference: Passives

In passive sentences, the object of the active verb becomes the subject of the passive verb. We can mention the person or thing ("agent") which performs the action, but it's not necessary.

		subject	verb	object
Active	In 1974,	a revolutionary political group	kidnapped	Patty Hearst.

		subject	verb	by	agent
Passive	In 1974,	Patty Hearst	was kidnapped	by	a revolutionary political group.

We use the passive when we want to say what happened to a subject rather than what a subject did.

*Patty Hearst **was renamed** "Tania."*   *Where **was** Che Guevara **killed**?*
*Korda's photos **were exhibited** in Paris in Spring 2001.*

How "Green" Is the Class?

Report writing

1 Work in small groups. Look at the activities below and discuss which ones are good and which are bad for the environment.

a) Traveling into a city by car.
b) Buying fresh, organic fruit or vegetables.
c) Using public transportation.
d) Taking bottles to a recycling center.
e) Recycling paper.
f) Wearing a fur coat.
g) Picking up litter and throwing it away.
h) Buying a hamburger in a plastic container.
i) Paying more for something because it is environmentally friendly.
j) Using plastic bags for your shopping.

2 Work in small groups. You are going to conduct a survey to find out how many people have done the activities in 1 in the last two weeks. Follow these instructions.

a) Prepare the question you are going to ask for each activity.
For example: a) *Have you traveled into a big city by car in the last two weeks?*
b) Decide who is going to ask which questions.
c) Go around the class and ask the questions and write down the answers.
d) In your groups, write down the results of the survey for each activity.

3 Using the results from 2, write a survey report which is true for your class by replacing the underlined expressions in the model text on the right. Change other parts of the model if necessary.

Survey Report

A survey was carried out in <u>Newtown, California</u>, to find out how green people are.

The results of the survey
5   show that <u>only a few people</u> have used public transportation in the last two weeks, but <u>everybody</u> has traveled into a city by car.

<u>Most of the people</u>
10   <u>interviewed</u> have bought a hamburger in a plastic container, and <u>several people</u> have picked up litter and thrown it away.

<u>A small number of people</u>
15   have taken bottles to a recycling center or have recycled paper, but <u>none of the people interviewed</u> have paid more for something because it is environmentally
20   friendly.

<u>A large number of people</u> have worn a fur coat, and <u>everybody</u> has used plastic bags for their shopping.

25   <u>Nobody</u> has bought organic fruit or vegetables in the last two weeks.

The results of the survey suggest that the <u>inhabitants of</u>
30   <u>Newtown, California</u>, are <u>not very green</u>.

13 *Dance*

Reading

Complete the questionnaire and compare your answers with a partner.

Vocabulary: *on* and *at*

1 Test your prepositions! The questionnaire talks about being *on stage* or *at a club*. Add *on* or *at* to each noun phrase in the box.

> the phone   a concert   vacation
> a plane   the doctor's   the Internet
> a business trip   the hairdresser's
> a dance club   a trip

on the phone,…   at a concert,…

2 Write down two true sentences and one false sentence about yourself, using prepositions + noun phrases in 1. Read your partner's sentences and guess which sentence is false.

> 1   *I was on the phone just before the class began.*
> 2   *I was at a dance club on Saturday.*
> 3   *I was…*

DANCE DIVA OR TWO LEFT FEET?

1 Your favorite place for dancing is…
   a on stage.
   b at a club or a party.
   c in your own bedroom.

2 Check the music you know how to dance to.
   ✓ Pop   ✓ Rock 'n' roll   House
   Reggae   ✓ Salsa   Flamenco
   Ballroom (e.g., waltz)
   Traditional music of your country

3 Which sentence best describes your attitude toward dancing?
   a I hate it.
   b I love it, and I'm pretty good.
   c I love dancing, but I'm not particularly good.

4 Which sentence best describes the way you dance?
   a I don't care what other people think.
   b I feel uncomfortable.
   c I want people to look at me.

5 When I dance,…
   a I stay more or less in one place.
   b I need a lot of room to move around.
   c I do the same as my partner.

6 At a pop concert, I usually…
   a get up and dance to the music.
   b stay sitting down.
   c I don't go to pop concerts.

7 How often do you dance all night?
   a About once or twice a year.
   b Never. Don't be ridiculous!
   c Every weekend.

8 At a party,…
   a I'm usually the last to get up and dance.
   b I'm usually the first to get up and dance.
   c I don't go to parties where people dance.

How to score
1 a 3, b 2, c 1   5 a 2, b 3, c 1
2 1 point for each check   6 a 3, b 2, c 1
3 a 1, b 3, c 2   7 a 2, b 1, c 3
4 a 3, b 1, c 2   8 a 2, b 3, c 1
Turn to page B124 to find out what your score means.

The Clubbing Capital of the World

Work in small groups. Discuss the questions.

- Which town or city in your country is famous for its nightlife?
- Where do people go dancing or clubbing where you live?
- Which is your own favorite place for a night out?

Reading

1 You are going to read an article about the island of Ibiza. Read the first part of the article (*Party Island*) and answer the questions.

a) What kind of people go to Ibiza? *turists*

b) How many tourists visit the island every year? *2½ mil*

c) How long has Ibiza been a party island? *1960s*

d) What happened in 1987?

e) What kinds of music do the DJs play?

Party Island

The beautiful Mediterranean island of Ibiza has a population of 80,000. But in the summer, two million tourists visit the island. Why? Because Ibiza is the clubbing capital of the world.

Top DJs play the latest dance music in 400 clubs and bars situated around the island's two main towns, San Antonio and Ibiza town.

Ibiza has been a party island since the sixties when hippies first started coming to the island.

But it became famous for clubbing with the arrival of Acid House in 1987.

Since then, DJs have been playing dance music for all tastes: dance, trance, techno, garage, pop, rock, funk, etc.

Ibiza

2 Have you ever been to a club that has any of the following? Compare with your partner.

a) live music

b) several different dance floors

c) foam parties

d) room for 10,000 people

e) a swimming pool

f) trees planted inside

3 Read the second part of the article (*The Clubs*). Match the clubs with the features in 2.

For example: a) live music – *Privilege*

The Clubs

Amnesia

(www.amnesia.es)

When it opened in the 70s, *Amnesia* had an open-air dance floor, but in 1990, noise laws forced the owners to build walls and a roof. The club is best-known for its foam parties. The music is a mix of house and trance, with some rock and pop. *Amnesia* has always been one of the island's favorite clubs for end-of-season parties.

Privilege

(www.privilege-ibiza.com)

The owners of a restaurant called *Ku* decided to build a mini disco (125 people maximum) back in 1978. It was here that Bob Marley, Grace Jones, and Freddie Mercury performed live, and many international stars have followed in their footsteps since then. In 1994, they built a new club and called it *Privilege*. It is the size of a soccer field—it has room for 10,000 and has everything: several different dance floors, palm trees in the main room, a DJ suspended over the swimming pool, and on some nights there's even a DJ in the restrooms!

4 Would you like to go to Ibiza? Why/Why not? Tell your partner.

My Ibiza

Listening

1 Work with a partner. You are going to listen to a radio program called *My Ibiza*. Look at the photos of the three people interviewed and guess who said each of the following.

a) "I haven't been home in a couple of years now."
b) "I've been living in Ibiza since 1995." ~~5~~ S
c) "I've spent all my money." J
d) "I haven't been to the beach yet."
e) "I've been a resident DJ at *Amnesia* for two years." S
f) "I've been dancing all night." J

2 🔲 57 Listen and check your answers to 1. Which person do you think enjoys his/her life most?

Vocabulary: informal language

1 Replace the <u>underlined</u> words in these statements with informal expressions from the interview with Josh.

how come   I'm broke   beat   clubbing   reckon

a) I'm usually so <u>tired</u> after a night out that I don't get up till after lunch. *beat*
b) I often wonder <u>why</u> I never meet anybody interesting when I go out. *how come* , *clubbing*
reckon c) I've been <u>going to dance clubs</u> since I was fifteen.
d) I <u>think</u> it costs far too much to get into clubs these days.
e) When <u>I don't have any money</u>, I usually get my friends to pay for me. *I'm broke*

Ana E

beat = extremely tired

2 Find out if any of the statements in 1 are true for your partner.

Anecdote

Think of a time recently when you went to a place where people were dancing and having a good time. You are going to tell your partner about it. Choose from the list below the things you want to talk about. Think about what you are going to say and how you are going to say it.

☐ Where were you? A club? A party? A concert?
☐ What kind of music was playing?
☐ Who was playing the music? A live band? A DJ?
☐ How loud and clear was the music?
☐ How crowded was the place?
☐ What kind of clothes were people wearing?
☐ Did you dance or did you watch other people dancing?
☐ Were people dancing alone or with a partner?
☐ How long did you stay there?
☐ Did you have a good time?

▲ Josh, 18, student

▲ Simone, 29, DJ

▲ Antonio, 36, restaurant owner

Close-up

for and since

Language Reference p. 80

1 Look at the way *for* and *since* are explained in the diagram. Then complete the chart so that the information is correct counting from today.

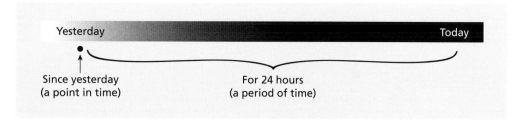

	Since		For
yesterday	=		*24 hours*
1999	=		*since years*
Sunday	=		*since day(s)*
my last birthday	=		___
I started studying English	=		___

2 Add more examples of your own to the chart in 1.

been and gone

Language Reference p. 80

1 Work with a partner. Read the following sentences about the people in the radio program *My Ibiza* on page 78. Then discuss the questions.

1 Josh <u>has been</u> in Ibiza for nine or ten days, but he <u>hasn't been</u> to the beach yet.
2 Simone <u>has been</u> in Ibiza since 1997. She is Brazilian, but she <u>hasn't been</u> home in a couple of years.

a) What tense are the <u>underlined</u> verbs?
b) In which case is *been* used to mean the same as *gone*?

2 Make true sentences about yourself, using the following cues and an appropriate time expression with *since*, *in*, or *never*. Compare your answers with a partner.

a) not go to a dance club
   For example: *I haven't gone to a dance club since I was twenty-four./I haven't gone to a dance club in years./I've never gone to a dance club!*
b) not go to a good party
c) not go to the beach
d) not go to a rock concert
e) not go to a wedding
f) not go out for dinner
g) not go skiing
h) not go abroad

David likes going somewhere hot for his vacations.

3 Write down the names of some good stores, restaurants, bars, or dance clubs in your city. Ask your partner if he/she knows them or has gone to them recently. Find out as much as you can.

STUDENT A

Have you ever gone to *Monsoon*?
Or
Have you gone to *Monsoon* recently?

STUDENT B

Yeah, I went there last Saturday.
Or
No, never. What / Where is it?

1 Look at the chart based on information from the radio program *My Ibiza* on page 78. Which "facts" tell us *how long* an activity has continued?

1 Past facts	+	**2 Present facts**	→	**3 Present perfect facts**
Simone started as a DJ at *Amnesia* two years ago.	+	Simone is a DJ at *Amnesia*.	→	She's been a DJ at *Amnesia* for two years.
Tourists started coming to Ibiza in the sixties.	+	Tourists come to Ibiza every year.	→	They've been coming to Ibiza since the sixties.

2 Underline the main verbs in column 3 of the chart in 1. Discuss these questions with your partner.

a) Which verb describes a state?
b) Is it in the present perfect or present perfect continuous?
c) Which verb describes a single or repeated action?
d) Is it in the present perfect or present perfect continuous?

3 Write the name of…

a) a foreign person you <u>know</u>.
b) a type of music you <u>like</u>.
c) a subject you <u>are</u> interested in.
d) a club or bar you <u>go</u> to.
e) a store you <u>buy</u> clothes in.
f) a favorite possession you <u>have</u>.
g) the house you <u>live</u> in.
h) the place you <u>work</u> or <u>study</u>.

1 Decide if each <u>underlined</u> verb describes a state or a single/repeated action.
2 Write eight present perfect facts which answer the question *How long…?*
3 Compare your facts with a partner.

For example: *I've known Max for seven years. I've been going to Bar Isa since 1999.*

4 Work as a class. Find out who has done or who has been doing the things in 3 the longest. Follow these instructions.

a) Each student choose one "fact" from 3 and practice the questions you will ask. For example: *a) Do you know anybody foreign?* → *How long have you known him/her?*
b) Ask everybody in the class and record the answers.
c) Report the results back to the class.

Language Reference: Present perfect and present perfect continuous

for and *since*

for + a period of time and *since* + a point in time are two ways of saying the same thing.

for a few days / for three years / for ages
since Monday / since I graduated / since 1997

been and *gone*

The past participle of *go* is *gone*; *been* is the past participle of *be*. However, *been* is sometimes used to mean the same as *gone*.

He **hasn't been** to the beach yet. (go)
Have you **been** abroad this year? (go)
I've been sick since last night. (be)
How long **have you been** here? (be)

Present perfect and present perfect continuous

We can use the present perfect when we want to say how long something has continued from a point in the past up to now. For verbs with stative meanings, we always use the present perfect.

I've been a DJ for two years.
She's known Tommy since they were in school.

For verbs with dynamic meanings, we usually use the continuous form.

I've been clubbing every night.
My mother's **been playing** tennis since she was eight.

Note: We can use the present perfect for unchanging, permanent situations and the present perfect continuous for temporary situations. Compare:

I've lived here all my life. (Permanent)
I've been living here since May. (Temporary)

Billy Elliot

Reading and listening

1 Read this introduction to an excerpt from a book based on the movie *Billy Elliot*. What is the problem? What do you think will happen?

> Billy's mother is dead. His father and brother are miners, and they are on strike. Billy's father wants his son to learn to box, like he did and his father before him, but Billy becomes fascinated by the magic of ballet. In secret, Billy starts taking ballet lessons every Saturday. In this excerpt from the story, Billy describes what happens when his father comes to watch him boxing but instead finds him in a ballet class.

2 🎞 58 Read and listen to the excerpt. Who do you sympathize with: Billy or his dad?

nan (line 6): informal word for *grandmother*

telly (line 7): informal word for *television*

wind me up (line 10): informal expression for *annoy me*

lads (line 15) informal word for *boys*

I had him there (line 17): informal expression for *caught him in a difficult situation*

(From *Billy Elliot*, by Melvin Burgess)

Back home he pointed at a chair behind the table, staring at me all the while he was taking his coat off. Then he sat down opposite me.

I knew what he wanted. He wanted me to say sorry. Well, I wasn't going to. He could wait for ever. It was stupid! What had I done wrong?

5 "Ballet," he said at last.

"So what's wrong with ballet?" I said. My nan was sitting on a chair by the window, eating a pork pie and watching us like we were on the telly. I looked at her. It was easier than having to look at him. I could see him turning red again out of the corner of my eye.

10 "What's wrong with ballet? Look at me, Billy. Are you trying to wind me up?"

"It's perfectly normal," I said, turning to face him.

"Normal?" I was scared. He'd gone all white around the lips.

"I used to go to ballet," said my nan.

"See?" I said.

15 "For your nan. For girls, Billy. Not for lads. Lads do football or boxing or wrestling or something."

"What lads do wrestling?" I asked and I had him there because no one I know does wrestling round here.

"You know what I mean."

20 "I don't know what you mean."

The thing is, all right, I knew what he meant. At least, I used to know. Ballet isn't what boys do. It's not football and boxing and being hard. It's not what we do. But once I've done it, it is what we do.

Just because I like dancing, it doesn't mean I'm turning into someone else.

25 Does it?

3 Here is a brief summary of the excerpt. Put the lines of the summary in the correct order.

( ) a) at his father. He looked
(2) b) off and without saying anything sat
( ) c) up. Billy knew what his father meant.
( ) d) down opposite Billy. Billy didn't look
(1) e) His father took his coat
( ) f) at his nan instead. Billy said there was nothing wrong
( ) g) with doing ballet, but his dad thought he was winding him

4 What interests did you have when you were twelve? What did you want to be? Tell your partner.

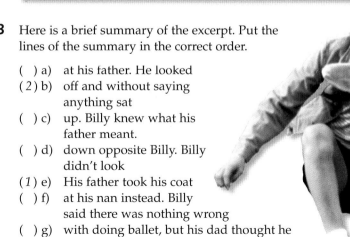

14 Call

Work in small groups. Discuss these questions.

- How many phone calls do you make/receive in a typical day?
- What do you use your phone for most?
- Who do you call most?

Reading **1** Work with a partner. List any things that you dislike about phones. Read the magazine article and check if it mentions any of the things on your list.

PHONE MOANS

Audrey: "I hate it when the person I'm speaking to starts drinking or eating something. It sounds disgusting!"

Ben: "It's so boring when you go out with somebody who spends half the time talking on her cell phone. When I go out with somebody, I turn my phone off and listen to my voice mail when I get home."

Cathy: "I think there should be places where cell phones are banned. For instance, when I'm on a train or in a restaurant, I hate listening to people talking about private things. It should be against the law! Call me old-fashioned, but I like to travel and eat in peace."

Dan: "I've given up calling my friends who have children. Every time I call them, they ask me to talk to their two-year-old boy. I have to speak to him in this silly voice, and he never talks, so I have to listen to him breathing into the phone. Luckily, they haven't asked me to talk to the baby yet, but she's usually screaming in the background, so you can't have a normal conversation anyway."

Ellen: "I like to talk to a real person on the phone, but nowadays you get a recorded message that gives you all these options to choose from. If you don't hear everything the first time, you can't ask them to repeat. You have to start again. Oh, and the music that they play while you're on hold—awful." terrible

Frank: "I hate it when you call a company or an office and you can never get through to the person you want to speak to. The operator connects you to an extension, and the person you want is not there, so you have to wait for ages. Then you get another extension, and it's still the wrong one, so you have to wait again. And again and again until you get tired of trying."

2 How many of the things mentioned in the article sometimes happen to you?

**Vocabulary:
telephones**

1 Complete the questions with words and expressions from the article on page 82.

a) Do you think it should be against the law to use a c_ell_ p_hone_ while you're driving?

b) Have you ever been in an embarrassing situation because you forgot to t____ your phone o_ff_ ?

c) When somebody leaves a message on your v_oice_ m_ail_ , how long do you wait before you return the call?

d) When was the last time you listened to a r_eco_rded m_essage_ and had to choose from different o_ption_?

e) While you are o_n_ h_old_, do you prefer to listen to music or to silence?

f) Have you ever had a problem getting connected to the right e_xtension_?

2 Choose three questions from 1 to ask your partner.

Domestic Crisis

Listening **1** ▪▪ 59 Listen to the first part of Lorna's telephone conversation. Which of the following problems does Lorna mention?

a) My back is hurting.

b) The house isn't clean.

c) The car has broken down.

d) The cat has died.

e) The kids are annoying me.

f) I've had a fight with my partner.

g) The refrigerator is empty.

h) I'm bored.

i) I don't have any money.

j) I've lost my keys.

2 Lorna uses the words and expressions in the box to talk about the five problems mentioned in 1. Rewrite the problems, using the words and expressions that Lorna uses. Listen and check your answers.

> a mess   run out of   killing me   nothing to eat   driving me crazy

3 ▪▪ 60 Listen to the second part of the telephone conversation. Who is Juliet?

4 ▪▪ 61 After the first conversation, Lorna tries to get help. She makes two more phone calls. Listen to the two conversations and say if each sentence is true (*T*) or false (*F*).

a) Lorna's mother is out. F

b) Lorna's father offers to help with the children. F

c) Lorna asks Jackie to baby-sit for a couple of hours. T

d) Jackie asks if her sister can come with her. F

e) Lorna offers to drive over and pick Jackie up. F

5 Have you ever had any of the problems in 1 above? Did you call anybody for help? Who? Tell your partner.

Close-up

I said, would you mind turning down your fan?

1 Listen again to Lorna's two conversations in 4 in the previous section. Match the opening phrases (a–g) with the sentence endings (1–7).

a) Can I

b) Should I 7

c) Could you 5

d) I was wondering if you could 2

e) Would you mind 6

f) Is it O.K. if I 3

g) Would you like me to 1

1 drive over and pick you up?

2 come over and baby-sit.

3 bring my boyfriend?

4 call you back later?

5 tell her it's urgent?

6 hanging on a minute, please?

7 leave a message for your mother?

2 Put the opening phrases in 1 (a–g) into three groups.

Offers: asking people if we can do something for them

Requests: asking people if they can do something for us

Requests for permission: asking people if it's O.K. for us to do something

b		
c		
a		

3 Work with a partner. Look again at the opening phrases in 1. Do you usually use more or fewer words if you want to be formal?

4 Look at the following mini-situations. Think of a person you would call for each situation. Tell your partner.

A
You want someone to choose a movie for you to see together.

B
You want someone to take care of your pet while you are on vacation.

C
You want someone to write a job reference for you.

D
You want someone to check an important letter you've written in English.

E
You want someone to help you buy a new outfit for a friend's wedding.

F
You want someone to lend you some money till the end of the month.

5 Work with a partner. Choose two of the mini-situations in 4 and write a short phone conversation for each one. Include an offer and a request in each conversation.

Language Reference: Offers and requests

Offers

Here are two common ways of asking people if we can do something for them.
***Should I** give you a ride?*
***Would you like me to** help you?*

Requests

There are many ways of asking people if they can do something for us. Usually, the more words we use, the more polite or formal the request sounds.

***I was wondering if you could**…?* ↑ more polite/formal
***Would you mind**…?*
***Could you**…?* ↓ more direct/informal

Here are some ways we can request permission—ask people if it is O.K. for us to do something.
***Can I** use your phone, please?*
***Is it O.K. if I** bring my friend?*

Telephone Talk

Listening 1 Lorna finally tries to get in touch with her husband at work. He works for a company called Butler and Crowmarch. Complete her conversation with the receptionist, using the most appropriate expressions.

> R: (1) **Yes / Good morning**. Butler and Crowmarch.
> L: (2) **Could I / I want to** speak to Mr. Carr, please?
> R: Certainly. (3) **Who's calling, please? / Who are you?**
> L: Mrs. Carr.
> R: (4) **Wait / One moment, please.**
> Hello. (5) **He's not there. / I'm sorry, but Mr. Carr is away from his desk.**
> L: Oh. (6) **Do you know when he'll / When will he** be back?
> R: I'm not sure. (7) **Would you like / Do you want** me to ask his assistant?
> L: Yes, please.
> R: Just a moment, please. (8) **He's busy till five. / Hello, Mrs. Carr. Mr. Carr is in a meeting until five o'clock.**
> L: Oh, O.K. (9) **Can I / Let me** leave a message.
> R: Certainly.
> L: (10) **Tell him / Could you tell him** to call me before he leaves the office? It's important.
> R: No problem, Mrs. Carr. I'll give him the message.
> L: Thank you. Goodbye.

2 ▭ **62** Listen and compare your version with the version on the recording.

3 Work with a partner. Practice the conversation. Take turns being Lorna and the receptionist.

Telephone numbers 1 ▭ **63** The following telephone numbers have been copied down incorrectly. Listen to the recording and correct the numbers.

a) Amtrak train schedules and fares:
   1 (900) 872-7245
b) Budget Rent-A-Car: 1 (728) 656-6010
c) AAA emergency road service:
   1 (800) 222-3457

d) Port Authority bus schedules:
   1 (212) 500-2341
e) PATH Trains to New Jersey:
   1 (800) 234-6624
f) Directory Assistance: 401

2 Explain your answers in 1 to a partner. Take turns identifying the mistake and saying what the correct number is. Do not show each other any numbers you have written down.

For example: *For Amtrak trains, it isn't one nine hundred. It's one eight hundred. Do you agree?*

3 Work with a partner and complete the following task.

a) Write down five telephone numbers that are important to you.
b) Take turns dictating the numbers to each other.
c) Check that you wrote down your partner's numbers correctly.
d) Explain to each other why the numbers are important.

The "Latest Thing"

1 You are going to read an article about a father who doesn't want to buy a cell phone for his twelve-year-old son. Why do you think he does not want his son to have a phone? Discuss with a partner. Read the article. Are any of your ideas mentioned?

Why I Bought My Child a Gun

Every five minutes my children ask me for the "latest thing." They tell me that all their friends have it already, and they can't live without it. Our house is full of Game Boys, Play
5 Station CDs, and a million other "latest things."
  But the one "latest thing" we have refused to buy is a cell phone. Our twelve-year-old wants one, and we've said "no." He says he'll use it only for messaging and he really needs it for emergencies.
10 We don't want him to have a cell phone, because they may be bad for children's health. Unfortunately, when I say, "I don't want you to have a cell phone, because you might get a brain tumor," he tells me that he doesn't mind.

15 Why do twelve-year-old boys only want things that are bad for them? We've already told him that he can't listen to rap music—the words are disgusting. And I've said no to beer with his meals. Right now, I'm saying no to everything.
20 Then a few weeks ago he asked for something called a BB gun. He says everybody has one. Of course they do. He shows me a Web site full of them and tells me it fires only plastic pellets. Finally, I say yes. I can't believe I've said no to
25 phones and yes to guns.
  In October our son becomes a teenager, and I pray that research will find that cell phones
30 are safe ... even better, that they make young people less moody—and more interested in personal hygiene.
  Until then, I'm saying no.

(Adapted from the Guardian)

2 Work in small groups. Discuss the following questions.

- Who is the youngest person you know with a cell phone?
- What are the arguments for and against letting young children have cell phones?
- At what age do you think it's O.K. for children to have cell phones?

Vocabulary:
say, tell, ask

I can't talk now.

1 Complete this summary of the article by choosing the most appropriate alternative.

a) The father's twelve-year-old son always **says/tells/asks** him for the "latest thing."
b) He **says/~~tells~~/asks** him that he wants a cell phone.
c) He **~~says~~/tells/asks** that he'll use it only for messaging.
d) He **says/~~tells~~/asks** him that he doesn't mind getting a brain tumor.
e) The son then **says/tells/~~asks~~** for a BB gun.
f) He **~~says~~/tells/asks** everybody has one.
g) He **says/~~tells~~/asks** him it fires only plastic pellets.
h) The father **~~says~~/tells/asks** "no" to the cell phone and "yes" to the gun.

2 Complete each of the following rules with *say, tell,* or *ask*.

a) You ask (somebody) for something.
b) You tell somebody something.
c) You say something.

Who? What? Where?

1 🔲 **64** You are going to listen to six short conversations. Listen and answer these questions: Who is speaking? What is the situation? Where are they? Choose from the places in the box.

in a parking garage   at a club   at a bus stop   at home   at the zoo   at home

2 Which of the situations in 1 have you been in? Tell your partner.

Close-up

Indirect questions

1 Work with a partner. Look at the position of subject and verb in these sentences and discuss the questions below.

Direct questions   **Indirect questions**

be

question word	verb	subject		question frame	subject	verb	
Where	is	the restroom	? →	Do you know where	the restroom	is	?

Other verbs

question word	auxiliary	subject	verb		question frame	subject	verb	
–	Has	the last bus	left	? →	Do you know if	the last bus	has left	?

a) Where does the subject go in direct questions with *be*?
b) Where does the subject go in direct questions with other verbs?
c) Where does the subject go in indirect questions?

2 Put the subjects in the correct position in these direct and indirect questions. Listen again to the six conversations and check your answers.

Subjects	Direct questions	Indirect questions
a) the restroom	Where is *the restroom*?	Could you tell me where *the restroom* is?
b) the time	What is?	Do you have any idea what is?
c) the lions	Where are?	Do you know where are?
d) I	Could have a Zoomatron?	Do you think could have a Zoomatron?
e) I	Where can get a taxi?	Do you know where can get a taxi?
f) we	Where did leave it?	Can you remember where left it?

3 Work with a partner. Rewrite the ends of these indirect questions in the correct order.

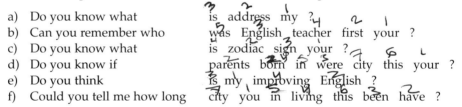

a) Do you know what   is address my ?
b) Can you remember who   was English teacher first your ?
c) Do you know what   is zodiac sign your ?
d) Do you know if   parents born in were city this your ?
e) Do you think   is my improving English ?
f) Could you tell me how long city you in living this been have ?

4 Ask each other the questions in 3.

Language Reference: Indirect questions

The word order in indirect questions is different from the word order in direct questions. It is the same as in normal statements: *subject + verb (+ object)*. You do not use the auxiliaries *do/does/did*.

Question frame	Subject	Verb	(Object)
Do you think	*I*	*could have*	*a Zoomatron?*
Do you know if	*the last bus*	*has left?*	
Can you remember who	*your first English teacher*	*was?*	
Could you tell me where	*you*	*live?*	

15

Review 3

The Waiting Game

Language reviewed: describing people (Unit 11); *for* and *since* (Unit 13); present perfect and present perfect continuous (Unit 13); indirect questions (Unit 14); noun phrases with *on* and *at* (Unit 13)

Listening

1 ▶ 65 You are going to listen to a radio reporter conduct three interviews with people in line to get tickets for the Wimbledon tennis championships. Look at the picture while you are listening and answer the questions.

a) Who thinks they will get into Wimbledon?
b) Who doesn't think they will get in?

Hyacinth | Derek | Maria | Oona | Sara

2 Rearrange the words to make the questions that the reporter asked in the first interview.

a) Could you tell me   come   from   where   you   ?
b) Could you tell me   been   have   how   long   waiting   you   ?
c) Do you think   get   in   you   will   ?
d) Do you know   are   how   in   many   front   people   of   there   you   ?

3 Listen to the first interview again and check the word order of the questions in 2. How does the woman answer the questions?

4 Complete the sentences from the interviews. Put each verb into the present perfect or the present perfect continuous and choose *for* or *since*.

a) You (**look**) at her **for/since** hours.   *You've been looking at her for hours.*
b) I (**wait**) here **for/since** eight fifteen this morning.
c) I (**be**) in London **for/since** four weeks.
d) It (**rain**) **for/since** one thirty.
e) We (**be**) here **for/since** about eight.
f) We (**chat**) **for/since** ages.

5 Listen to the interviews again to check your answers to 4.

6 Work in small groups. Which do you prefer:

a) watching big sporting events live?
b) watching big sporting events on TV?
c) not watching big sporting events?

Discuss your answers and give examples from your own experience.

1 Complete the descriptions with words from the box. Match each description to a person in the picture of the line for Wimbledon on page 88.

bags cheeks hard-working humor annoying miserable outfits teeth wavy wrinkled

A She has pale skin and a few freckles, but the most noticeable thing about her is her eyelashes. She doesn't have any! She always looks _____ , but in reality, she is not unhappy. She is serious and _____—and always extremely polite.

B She has short, gray _____ hair and always wears green to match her green eyes. Her _____ are always red—is it because she is embarrassed or does she suffer from the cold? Certainly, she is very shy, but she is a loyal friend and can be a lot of fun to be with.

C She's a senior citizen with a warm personality and a friendly face. Sociable and easygoing, she has a wonderful sense of _____ and seems to be smiling all the time. Even with her tanned, _____ face, she is still good-looking.

D He's fifty-two but looks older. With unwashed hair, big, bushy eyebrows, and a mustache that seems to have some of his dinner still in it, he's usually a mess. In fact, you could say that personal hygiene is not his strong point. He has _____ under his eyes because he doesn't sleep enough. He wears an old-fashioned suit (does he sleep in it?) and has an _____ habit of looking the other way when you talk to him.

E She's fifty, and she always likes to look her best when she goes out. She wears stylish _____ and chooses lipsticks to match. Red is her favorite color because it·shows off her row of beautiful pearly _____ . She recently dyed her hair pink. She is very sure of herself, and some people think she is kind of bossy.

2 On a piece of paper, write a short description of another student in your class. Fold your piece of paper and give it to your teacher. Then take a piece of paper with a description written by another student and guess who is being described.

1 Complete each sentence in the questionnaire with *at* or *on*.

HOW PATIENT ARE YOU?

1 You're _____ the Internet and downloading an interesting program, but it's very, very slow. How long will you wait before giving up?   _____ **minutes**

2 You are _____ a party _____ a friend's house. It's extremely boring, and you know only one person—your friend. How long will you wait before going home? _____ **minutes**

3 You are going _____ a business trip tomorrow, and you decide to have your hair cut before you go. It is very, very busy _____ the hairdresser's. How long will you wait before giving up?   _____ **minutes**

4 You're sitting _____ a plane, and the person _____ your right is listening to loud music _____ his personal stereo. How long will you wait before asking him to turn it down?
          _____ **minutes**

5 You are going out _____ a date. Your friend is waiting for you _____ the movie theater. You are _____ the bus stop, but your bus does not arrive. How long will you wait before calling a taxi _____ your cell phone?   _____ **minutes**

Total number of minutes: _____

2 Answer the questions in the questionnaire. For each question, write the maximum number of minutes that you will wait. When you have finished, add up the minutes for all the questions. Write your total.

3 Compare your answers with other people. Who is the most patient/impatient person in the class?

National Sports

Language reviewed: passives (Unit 12); dynamic and stative meanings (Unit 12); verb patterns (Unit 11); imperatives (Unit 11); say, tell, and ask (Unit 14); offers and requests (Unit 14); phrasal verbs (Unit 11)

Passives

1 Complete each of the following statements with an appropriate passive form of the verb. Then decide if the statements are true or false. Check your answers on page B125.

a) The 1992 Olympic games (**hold**) in Atlanta, Georgia. True or false?
b) Cricket (**play**) by two teams of thirteen players. True or false?
c) The game of rugby (**invent**) at Rugby School, England in 1823. True or false?
d) Mount Everest (**climb**) for the first time in 1953. True or false?
e) Bob Beamon's 1968 long jump world record of 8.9 meters (**never break**). True or false?
f) Brazil (**beat**) 2–1 by Germany in the 2002 soccer World Cup final. True or false?

2 Make up three more true/false statements about trivia, using passive verb structures. Exchange your statements with your partner. Are they true or false?

Dynamic and stative meanings

1 You are going to look at some pictures of a London street. Before you look at the pictures, choose the best verb forms in the questions below.

a) What **happens/is happening** in your picture?
b) How **do the people stand/are the people standing**?
c) What **do they wear/are they wearing**?
d) What **do they have/are they having** in their hands?
e) Where **do you think/are you thinking** the people **come/are coming** from? Why?

2 Work with a partner. Student A, look at the picture on page B124. Student B, look at the picture on page B126. Discuss the questions in 1. How many similarities and differences can you find between the pictures?

Reading

1 Read the article below about lining up or "queuing" in Britain. Choose either the *to*-infinitive or the *-ing* form for the verbs in parentheses. How useful is the advice in the article?

The Noble Art of Lining Up

There is one sport at which the British are always the world champions. Nobody can beat them at the noble art of lining up, or as they say, "queuing." The British actually look forward to (1 **spend**) their weekends in a line, or queue, waiting for a store to open or waiting for a parking space at the furniture superstore.

If you ever decide (2 **visit**) Britain, you will need (3 **know**) some of the basic rules of the sport.

First of all, remember that you need only one person to form a line. If you are alone at a bus stop, for example, don't look too relaxed. Make sure that you are in the line, and look optimistically to your right.

If you want (4 **keep**) your place in the line, never leave a space between you and the person in front; otherwise the person behind you will ask, "Are you in the queue?" (meaning "Don't you know how to queue properly?").

Conversation is generally not a good idea, and only two topics are acceptable: the weather and the bus schedule. Anything more and you will end up with a complete stranger sitting next to you, telling you his or her life story.

Unfortunately, the bus does not always stop in the correct place. Try (5 **stay**) calm and, whatever you do, don't cut in line, or as they say in Britain, "jump the queue." You can be sure that every single person in the line knows exactly who is in front of them and who is behind.

Follow these simple rules and you, too, can enjoy (6 **visit**) the home of the noble art of lining up. But if you decide not to follow the rules, be prepared for the worst.

2 ▬ 66 Listen and check your answers.

3 Work with a partner. Complete the following task.

a) Underline all the examples of imperatives you can find in the article.
b) Prepare a list of useful "do's" and "don'ts" for foreign visitors to your country (e.g., driving; using public transportation; eating out; visiting someone's home).
c) Compare your list with other people in the class.

Vocabulary: telephone language

1 Have you ever been late for work, a meeting, an appointment, or a lesson? What did you say? Tell your partner.

2 Look at the outline of a telephone conversation. Choose the correct word in each sentence.

MRS. KNIGHTLY

1 Mrs. Knightly **asks/tells** for Mr. Rogers.

4 Mrs. Knightly **asks/tells** the secretary if she will take a message.

6 Mrs. Knightly **says/tells** the secretary her name.
7 She **says/tells** she will be late.

9 Mrs. Knightly **tells/says** no.
10 She **tells/says** she'll call back later.

THE SECRETARY

2 The secretary **says/asks** Mrs. Knightly to wait.

3 She **says/tells** that Mr. Rogers is not there.

5 The secretary **says/tells** yes.

8 The secretary **asks/tells** Mrs. Knightly for her telephone number.

3 Match the stages (*1–10*) in the telephone conversation in 2 with the speeches (*a–j*) below.

a) Uh, would you mind taking a message?
b) Certainly. Could you hold for a minute, please?
c) Certainly.
d) I'll call back later.
e) Uhm, well, it's Joanna Knightly.
f) I'm sorry, but Mr. Rogers is not in yet, ma'am.
g) I have an appointment with Mr. Rogers at 9:15, and I'm sorry, but I missed the bus…
h) Oh, hello. Can I speak to Mr. Rogers, please?
i) That's all right, thanks.
j) Would you like to give me your telephone number, and I'll ask Mr. Rogers to call you when he gets in?

4 🔊 **67** Listen to the conversation to check your answers. Practice the conversation with a partner.

Vocabulary: phrasal verbs

1 Complete the sentences with words from the box.

| down   out   out   over   off   up   up |

a) My car broke ＿＿＿ last night.
b) I turned ＿＿＿ my cell phone, so I didn't get your message about the meeting.
c) I went ＿＿＿ with some friends last night, so I went to bed very late and overslept this morning.
d) The bus ran ＿＿＿ of gas, and we're waiting for another one to arrive.
e) A friend said that she would pick me ＿＿＿ in her car, but she hasn't arrived yet.
f) I split ＿＿＿ with my boy/girlfriend last night, and I need a little time to get ＿＿＿ it.

2 Work with a partner. Discuss these questions.

• Which sentence in 1 is the best excuse for being late?
• Which is the worst excuse?
• What other excuses can you think of?

3 Work with a partner. Write and practice a telephone conversation between a person who is late for work and his/her boss.

Review 3 UNIT 15 **91**

Nightclubs

Language reviewed: informal language (Unit 13); modals of obligation and permission (Unit 9); clothes and accessories (Unit 6)

1 Work in groups of four. Discuss the following questions.

- How many good nightclubs are there in your city?
- Which is the most expensive club to get into?
- Have you or your friends ever had difficulty getting into a club? Why?

2 Look at these pictures of the scene and the characters in a sketch called *The Door*. Compare the pictures to your favorite nightclub and the kind of people who go there. How different are they? Tell your partner.

3 🔲 68 You are going to listen to and read the sketch. What do the bouncers do so that they can go home early?

4 Work in groups of four. You are going to perform the sketch.

a) Decide who is going to play each character. (The first man, second man, and third man can be played by the same person. The first woman and second woman can be played by the same person.)

b) Practice your parts individually. Think about what voice your character will have, what he/she will look like, and how he/she will act.

c) Perform the sketch for the rest of the class.

The Door

Scene   Outside a nightclub. Two bouncers, B1 and B2, one on either side of the door. Music coming out of the club.

Characters **B1** (Bouncer 1)
5   **B2** (Bouncer 2)
                  M1 (First man)
                  W1 (First woman)
                  M2 (Second man)
                  W2 (Second woman)
10   **M3** (Third man)

B1 You O.K., pal?

B2 Yeah.

B1 You look beat—what have you been up to?

B2 I *am* beat—I've worked every night this week.

15 **B1** What? You're crazy.

B2 Yeah, but I'm broke. I need the cash. I'm looking forward to getting home tonight though—know what I mean?

B1 Cheer up—it's midnight, and there's hardly
20 anybody here. I guess we can finish early tonight.

B2 No—look, people are starting to arrive now.

B1 Don't worry—we'll get rid of them soon.

First man approaches.

B1 Sorry, pal, you can't come in.

25 **M1** What do you mean I can't come in?

B1 Sorry, pal. We have a very strict dress code here, and you can't come in.

M1 Why not?

B1 Because you're wearing sneakers.

30 **M1** But I was here last night, and I was wearing exactly the same clothes.

B1 Last night was "casual night." Tonight is "dress casual" night.

M1 Dress casual night? What are you talking about?

35 **B1** On dress casual night, you have to wear dress casual clothes. You can't wear jeans, sneakers, or baseball caps.

M1 Well, I'm not coming here again.

First woman approaches.

40 **B1** Sorry, beautiful, you can't come in.

W1 What?

B2 Sorry, but we have a very strict dress code here, and you can't come in.

W1 But I'm a model. You have to let me in.

45 **B1** Yeah, but we can't let you in. You're wearing jeans.

W1 But they're designer jeans. I paid a lot of money for them. Everybody wears jeans.

B2 Yeah, but rules are rules. You can't come in.

W1 I'm going to tell all my friends about this.

50 *Second man approaches.*

B2 Sorry, pal, you can't come in.

M2 What?

B1 Sorry, but we have a very strict dress code here, and you can't come in.

55 **M2** But I'm wearing a suit.

B2 That's right. It's dress casual night, and you're wearing a suit, so you can't come in.

M2 But I came here on Monday night, and I was wearing exactly the same clothes.

60 **B1** Monday night was formal night, sir. On formal night you have to wear a suit.

B2 Yeah, tonight is dress casual night, and you have to wear dress casual clothes.

M2 How ridiculous. I'm not coming here again.

65 *Second woman approaches.*

B1 Sorry, miss, but you can't come in.

W2 Why not? I'm twenty-one.

B2 Sorry, miss, but we have a very strict dress code, and you can't come in.

70 **W2** But I'm not wearing sneakers or jeans or a baseball cap.

B1 No, but your skirt's too short. You can't wear a miniskirt on dress casual night.

W2 Look, I'm the DJ's girlfriend. You have to let me in.

75 **B2** Yeah, and I'm the DJ's brother-in-law. Now get lost!

W2 Oh, yeah? I'll see you later.

Third man approaches.

B1 Evening, sir.

80 **M3** Evening.

B2 All right, you can go in.

Almost immediately the third man comes out.

B1 That was quick, sir.

M3 It's too boring—there's nobody in there!

85 **B1** O.K. Let's go home.

B2 All right, pal. See you tomorrow.

Lifestyle

Reading

1 Work with a partner. Choose an appropriate alternative to give somebody advice on how to live longer. Decide on the top three tips for a healthy and longer life.

You'll live longer if you ...
a) eat a low- **calorie**/**vitamin**/**protein** diet.
b) eat three quarters **junk**/**frozen**/**plant** food and one quarter **animal**/**canned**/**baby** food.
c) eat seven servings of **jam**/**fruit and vegetables**/**chocolate** every day.
d) stop eating when you are **50%**/**80%**/**100%** full.
e) do the things you **enjoy**/**hate**/**can**.
f) have a strong network of **advisors**/**friends**/**doctors**.

2 Read this article about the lifestyle on the island of Okinawa in Japan. Which tips from 1 are mentioned?

How Not to Die Before You Get Old

Chiako is active and healthy. She gets up at 7 A.M. every day, takes a brisk 30-minute walk, and plays gate-ball with her friends three times a week. There is nothing unusual about this, except that Chiako is 102 years old. She is not alone—there are hundreds of healthy
5 centenarians who lead similar lives in Okinawa.

Okinawa is a group of islands between Japan and Taiwan. Near a beach, there is a large stone with the following words on it: "At 70 you are still a child, at 80 you are just a youth, and at 90, if the ancestors invite you into heaven, ask them to wait until you are 100, and then
10 you might consider it."

Okinawans manage to stay thin in old age by eating a low-calorie diet that consists of three quarters plant food and one quarter animal food. They eat seven servings of fruit and vegetables every day, and they stop eating when they are 80% full.

15 They also keep active by dancing, walking, and gardening. In other words, they do the things they enjoy.

Okinawans have developed a stress-resistant personality. Nobody is in a hurry, schedules are non-existent, and there is always tomorrow. Hundreds of people, both young and old, go to the beach every day
20 to watch the spectacular sunsets. In Okinawa, there is always time to watch the sun set.

As well as large extended families, Okinawans have strong networks of friends. "When someone is ill and doesn't come to work, a neighbor will always knock on the person's door to find out how he or she is."

25 There's no magic pill. If you have good friends, a healthy diet, and a stress-free lifestyle, you will live longer. It's as simple as that!

3 How different is your lifestyle from the one described on Okinawa? Compare with your partner.

1 Complete these expressions with words from the article on Okinawa.

a) How often do you go for a b*risk* walk?
b) Do you think you h*ave* a healthy lifestyle?
c) Do you feel that you are always i*n* a hurry?
d) Do you have a large e*xtended* family?
e) Do you have a strong n*etwork* of friends?

2 Work with a partner. Ask each other the questions in 1.

Anecdote Think about the healthiest or fittest person you know. You are going to tell your partner about this person. Choose from the list the things you want to talk about. Think about what you will say and what language you will need.

☐ Is it a man or a woman?   ☐ What does he/she do for a living?
☐ How old is this person?   ☐ What does he/she do to stay healthy and fit?
☐ How do you know this person?   ☐ Has this person ever been unhealthy or unfit?
☐ What does he/she look like?   ☐ How is his/her lifestyle different from yours?

Health Spas

Listening **1** 🔊 69 You are going to listen to a woman asking for information about a health spa.

a) What's the name of the health spa?
b) Why does she want the information?
c) What do you think her husband will think about her idea?

2 Complete the sentences by choosing the correct alternatives and then listen to the conversation again. Check (✓) the activities that her husband will do at the health spa.

a) He'll **pass/take** a fitness test.   d) He'll **do/make** two hours of yoga.
b) He'll **make/go on** a diet.   e) He'll **do/have** a sauna.
c) He'll **take/have** a cigarette.   f) He'll **make/go for** a four-hour hike.

3 Work with a partner. Discuss these questions.

• Are there any health spas in your country like the one in the recording?
• What kind of people go to health spas?
• Would you like to go to one?

Close-up

Language Reference p. 97

Verb Structures p. B128

Future time clauses

1 Work with a partner. Look at the following sentences from the listening in the previous section and answer the questions.

Conjunction	+	Subordinate clause	+	Main clause
As soon as	+	*he arrives,*	+	*he'll take a fitness test.*
If	+	*he has a cigarette,*	+	*he'll be in big trouble.*
When	+	*he finishes the week,*	+	*he'll feel like a new man.*

a) Do these sentences refer to past, present, or future time?
b) Which verb structure is used in the main clause?
c) Which verb structure is used in the subordinate clause?

2 Which of the conjunctions in 1 suggests:

a) something will *possibly* happen?
b) something will *certainly* happen at a particular time?
c) something will happen *immediately*?

3 Look at how the sentences in 1 are formed. Is the following sentence structure also possible?

main clause + conjunction + subordinate clause (*He'll take a fitness test as soon as he arrives.*)

4 Complete each of these sentences with the correct verb structure.

a) If there's nothing good on TV tonight, I **go/'ll go** out.
b) When I **'ll go/go** on vacation next summer, I'll send you a postcard.
c) I'm going straight home as soon as the class **will end/ends**.
d) When I **'ll have/have** enough money, I'm going to buy a new jacket.
e) If I get up early tomorrow, I think I **go/'ll go** for a run.

5 How many sentences in 4 are true for you? Rewrite the sentences as necessary so that they are all true for you. Compare your sentences with a partner.

will for prediction

1 Complete each of these quotes by inserting *will* in the correct position. Match each quote with the person who you think made the prediction.

a) "Man *will* not fly for fifty years."	1 Bob Metcalf, founder of 3Com Corporation, in 1995. (A year later, he took his magazine article, liquefied it in a blender, and ate it with a spoon.)
b) "No woman in my time be Prime Minister."	2 Wilbur Wright to his brother Orville in 1901. (In 1903, the Wright brothers made the first flight.)
c) "The Internet collapse within a year."	3 Conservative politician Margaret Thatcher in 1969. (She became British Prime Minister in 1979.)

2 Work in small groups. You are going to consult the Oracle to find out things about your future. Turn to page B125 and follow the instructions. Compare your answers.

3 Think about the topics in the box and use the sentence beginnings to write about your life in the future. Compare with your partner.

| family children relationships health and fitness house job travel |
| possessions money spare time hair English |

I'll definitely… /I definitely won't…   I hope I'll… /I hope I won't…
I'll probably… /I probably won't…   I think I'll … /I don't think I'll…

Language Reference: Future forms

Future time clauses

When we are talking about the future, we use a future form in the main clause, but we use the simple present in the subordinate clause after *when, if, as soon as, before, after*, etc. We use a comma after the subordinate clause.

conjunction	subordinate clause	main clause
When	he **finishes** the week,	he'll feel like a new man.
If	he **has** a cigarette here,	he'll be in big trouble.

Note: Main clause + conjunction + subordinate clause (*He'll feel like a new man when he finishes the week.*) is an alternative order. We do not use a comma after the main clause.

will for prediction

We use *will* + simple verb form to make predictions about the future. We can grade or qualify our predictions by using the following structures.

I'll definitely / I definitely won't go to Mexico next summer.
My father will probably / My father probably won't retire when he's sixty-five.
I hope I'll / I hope I won't have more than two children.
I think I'll / I don't think I'll be rich and famous. NOT ~~I think I won't ...~~

Food Glorious Food

Vocabulary: food

Fruit and vegetables
oranges, lemons, bananas, apples, grapes, peaches, potatoes, tomatoes, lettuce, spinach, carrots, cauliflower, eggplant, mushrooms, red peppers, green beans, olives, cucumbers, onions, garlic
Meat, fish, and seafood
chicken, sausage, trout, sardines, shrimp
Other
tea, soup, nuts

1 Work with a partner. Look at the shopping list and check (✓) the items this person has bought. Which seven items has the person forgotten?

2 Place the items in 1 on the chart so they are true for you. Compare with your partner.

haven't had recently	have had recently	could live without	couldn't live without

3 Which of the items in 1 are never/always on your own shopping list? Add other things that are always on your shopping list. Compare with your partner.

Sounds and spelling

1 🔊 **70** The relationship between vowel sounds and spelling isn't always obvious. Listen and repeat the words in column A and column B.

A		B	
a)	lettuce	1	nut
b)	onion	2	tomato
c)	banana	3	spinach
d)	sardines	4	beans
e)	orange	5	lemon
f)	potato	6	olive

2 🔊 **71** Match a word from column A with a word from column B according to the **highlighted** vowel sounds. Listen and check your answers. Which word do you find most difficult to say?

Vocabulary: food idioms

1 Work with a partner. Look at the conversations and discuss.

a) Who do you think is speaking?
b) What do you think the conversations are about?

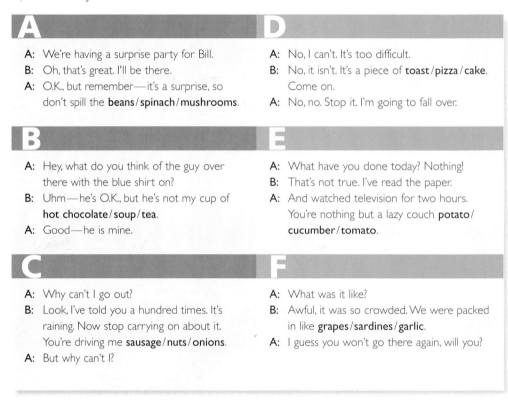

A

A: We're having a surprise party for Bill.
B: Oh, that's great. I'll be there.
A: O.K., but remember—it's a surprise, so don't spill the **beans/spinach/mushrooms**.

B

A: Hey, what do you think of the guy over there with the blue shirt on?
B: Uhm—he's O.K., but he's not my cup of **hot chocolate/soup/tea**.
A: Good—he is mine.

C

A: Why can't I go out?
B: Look, I've told you a hundred times. It's raining. Now stop carrying on about it. You're driving me **sausage/nuts/onions**.
A: But why can't I?

D

A: No, I can't. It's too difficult.
B: No, it isn't. It's a piece of **toast/pizza/cake**. Come on.
A: No, no. Stop it. I'm going to fall over.

E

A: What have you done today? Nothing!
B: That's not true. I've read the paper.
A: And watched television for two hours. You're nothing but a lazy couch **potato/cucumber/tomato**.

F

A: What was it like?
B: Awful, it was so crowded. We were packed in like **grapes/sardines/garlic**.
A: I guess you won't go there again, will you?

2 Complete the idioms by choosing the correct alternatives.

3 🔊 **72** Listen to the conversations and check your answers to 2. Do you have any idioms like these in your language?

4 Replace each <u>underlined</u> phrase with an idiom from 1.

a) I can't keep a secret—I always <u>tell everyone</u> about everything.
b) I could never be friends with <u>someone who watches TV all the time</u>.
c) I hate places where you are <u>with lots of other people</u>.
d) I think that learning English is <u>really easy</u>.
e) I was a naughty child and drove my parents <u>crazy</u>.
f) Going clubbing isn't <u>something I enjoy</u>.

5 Are the sentences in 4 true or false for you? Compare with a partner.

How to Eat a Banana

Vocabulary:
food
preparation

1 You are going to read an excerpt from a Web site about recipes for dishes made with bananas. Check (✓) the dishes you would like to try and put an ex (✗) next to the ones you wouldn't like to try.

2 Read the list of dishes again and write down words that describe:

    a) different ways of preparing food (For example: *peel*)

    b) different ways of cooking food (For example: *fry*)

    c) one word meaning *not cooked*

3 Think of lots of different items of food that you can prepare and cook in the ways described in 2.

    For example: *peel an apple, an orange, a potato*, etc. *fry an egg, fish, onions*, etc.

4 Think about a meal you have eaten recently. Write down exactly what you ate. How did the cook prepare the food? How did he/she cook the food? Describe the meal in detail to your partner.

17 *Animals*

Vocabulary: animals

Test your knowledge of animals! Work with a partner and match the definitions (*a–f*) with the words (*1–6*). The answers are on page B124.

Animal facts

a) An animal that can last longer without water than a camel.
b) A person who treats sick animals. 3
c) An insect that can lift fifty times its own weight. 5
d) An animal that can run at 60 mph. 1
e) An animal that can live to seventy years old. 6
f) An animal that can recognize its own image in a mirror. 2

1 A cheetah.
2 A dolphin.
3 A vet.
4 A giraffe.
5 An ant.
6 A turtle.

Homophones

1 There are some words in English that sound exactly the same but have different spellings and different meanings. Complete the chart by matching each of the words in the box with one of the clues below.

tail   weight   bear   right   deer   wait   dear   tale   write   bare

Word A	Sound	Word B
1 *tail* – a cat has a long one	/teil/	tale – an imaginative story
2 deer – brown animal with long legs/Bambi	/dir/	dear ...sir or madam,...
3 bear – a large animal with thick fur	/beir/	bare – empty/nude
4. right correct/not wrong	/rait/	write – use a pen to do this
5 wait – don't go/stay in one place	/weit/	weight – in pounds, for example

2 [cassette] 73 Listen, repeat, and check your answers. In your language, do you have words that sound the same but have different spellings?

Close-up

Relative clauses **1** Combine each of the following sentences with *that* to make one new sentence.

    a) I have a friend. He lives in San Diego. *I have a friend that lives in San Diego.*
    b) I have a car. It isn't very easy to park. *I have a car that isn't very easy to park*
    c) I know a woman. She has a beautiful singing voice. *I know a woman that has a beautiful*
    d) I went to a private school. ~~It~~ *that* was a long way from my house.
    e) My parents have two dogs. ~~They~~ *that* like going for long walks.
    f) I have a sister. ~~She~~ *that* works in a store.
    g) Last week I watched a very sad movie. ~~It~~ *that* made me cry.

2 Work with a partner. Look at the new sentences you have written in 1. <u>Underline</u> the relative clauses in the new sentences. What is the subject of the verb in each relative clause?

    For example: *I have a friend* | subject *that* | verb *lives* | *in San Diego.*

3 In which sentences in 1 can you replace *that* with *which*? In which sentences can you replace *that* with *who*? What is the rule for using the relative pronouns *which, who,* and *that*?

4 How many of the sentences in 1 are true for you? Compare your answers with a partner.

5 The definitions in column A are ungrammatical. Correct each one by ~~crossing out~~ one unnecessary word. Then match the definitions with a word from column B.

    A
    a) An animal that ~~it~~ can smell water three miles away.
    b) A person who ~~he~~ studies birds. 5
    c) An animal that ~~it~~ sleeps standing up. 7
    d) The only animal—apart from humans—that ~~it~~ gets sunburn 6
    e) A word to describe people who ~~they~~ are afraid of spiders. 8
    f) The thing that you sit on ~~it~~ when you ride a horse. 1
    g) An insect that you get malaria from ~~it~~. 3
    h) An animal whose name ~~it~~ means "I don't understand." 2

    B
    1 A saddle.
    2 A kangaroo.
    3 A mosquito.
    4 An elephant.
    5 An ornithologist.
    6 A pig.
    7 A horse.
    8 Arachnophobic.

6 Use the ideas in the boxes (and your own) to write down three true statements about your feelings or the feelings of people you know well. Compare your statements with a partner.

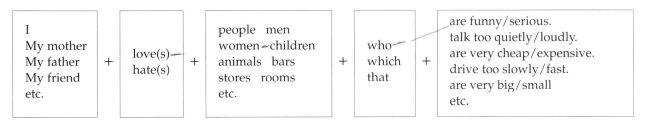

| I
My mother
My father
My friend
etc. | + | love(s)
hate(s) | + | people men
women children
animals bars
stores rooms
etc. | + | who
which
that | + | are funny/serious.
talk too quietly/loudly.
are very cheap/expensive.
drive too slowly/fast.
are very big/small
etc. |

Language Reference: Relative clauses

A *relative clause* gives additional information about a person or a thing introduced in the main clause. It comes immediately after the <u>person</u> or <u>thing</u> it is describing.

*A <u>person</u> **who treats sick animals** is called a vet.*
*I have a <u>car</u> **that isn't very easy to park**.*

We usually introduce a relative clause with a relative pronoun: **who** for people, **which** for things, and **that** for people or things. We usually use **which** only in written English and in formal spoken English. The relative pronoun becomes the subject (or the object) of the verb in the relative clause, so we don't need to use *she, him, it,* etc.

*An ornithologist is a person **who studies birds**.* NOT ... ~~who he studies birds~~
*A mosquito is an insect **that you get malaria from**.* NOT ... ~~that you get malaria from it~~

Animal Tales

Reading

1 Work in groups of three. You are going to read some true stories about the six animals in the pictures. Which animal do you think goes best with descriptions *A–F*?

A An animal that healed someone who was depressed.
B An animal that died of a broken heart.
C An animal that refused to be separated from another animal in the same house.
D An animal that knew when its owner was coming home.
E An animal that loved classical music.
F An animal that accidentally deleted some valuable files on a computer.

2 Work in groups of three. Student A, Student B, and Student C: Read your two animal stories and match a description in 1 to each story.

Student A

STORY 1

Mr. and Mrs. Roper live with their son, Robert, and a myna bird named Sammy. Robert travels a lot in his work, and he is sometimes away for weeks or even months. He doesn't always tell his parents when he is coming home, but he doesn't need to. Mr. and Mrs. Roper always know when their son is going to arrive because Sammy starts calling "Robbie" a few hours before Robert walks through the door.

STORY 2

Bill Bowell, a retired manager, was suffering from depression. The doctor gave him antidepressants, but they didn't help, and he was unable to work for twelve years.

Then he decided to swim with the dolphins.

"My life changed forever," says Bowell. "A dolphin named Simo looked into my eyes for a few minutes, and I started to cry. All my emotions erupted like a volcano. As I cried, Simo put his head on my chest and stayed very still." After swimming with dolphins, Bowell says he has fully recovered.

Student B

STORY 1

A man had to move to a new job a hundred twenty miles away. He owned a dog and a cat, and he loved them both. But he thought that the cat would prefer to stay in the same house with new owners.

So when he moved to a new house, he took only the dog.

About three weeks later, the dog suddenly disappeared. For several days, the man looked for his dog but didn't find him.

Then, seven weeks later, the dog showed up ... but he was not alone. By his side was the cat. They were tired and hungry after their long journey, and the cat's paws were bleeding. But they recovered quickly and were never separated again.

STORY 2

A bank worker in San Francisco decided to take his cat, Morris, into work with him one day. While the man was talking on the telephone, Morris walked across the keyboard of his computer and accidentally keyed in a secret code that deleted files worth $100,000. As you can imagine, the man's employers were not amused.

Student C

STORY 1

People say that fish are cold, but this story proves that they have feelings too.

A friend was moving to another country, so we took her pet goldfish and put it in a bowl with our goldfish. They lived together for six months, and when the friend came back, we separated them, and she took her goldfish home.

I immediately noticed that my goldfish was behaving strangely, banging against the side of the bowl. The next morning he was floating on the surface, dead.

Later that day, my friend called to say that her goldfish was also dead.

I believe they each died of a broken heart.

STORY 2

While on a camping trip a few years ago, my husband and I stopped in a quiet place for a picnic and played some Mozart on a CD player. After a few minutes, we looked up and realized that we were surrounded by cows who were listening to the music. When the Mozart was finished, we put on a CD of modern music. The cows immediately turned around and walked away.

3 Work in groups of three. Without looking at the book, take turns retelling your stories to the other people in your group. Explain which descriptions from 1 you have matched to your stories. Which story do you like best?

Vocabulary

1 The words and expressions in the box are from the stories in the previous section. Use them to complete this joke about a smart dog.

> showed up   turned around   paw   decided to   stayed very still   walked away
> looked into his eyes

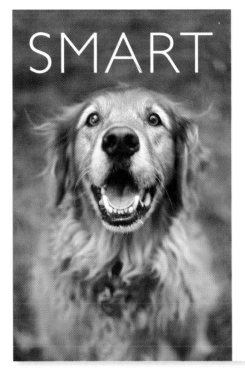

SMART DOG

For years, a dog (1) **showed up** on the butcher's doorstep every Wednesday morning to do his owner's shopping. On this Wednesday morning, the dog walked into the butcher's shop as usual with a purse around his neck. The butcher asked the dog what he wanted. He pointed his (2) ____ at the sausages. "How many pounds?" the butcher asked him. The dog (3) ____ and barked twice. The butcher packed two pounds of sausage. "Anything else?" he asked. The dog pointed to the hamburgers. "How many?" the butcher asked him. The dog barked four times, and the butcher packed four hamburgers. The dog then walked behind the counter and (4) ____ so the butcher could open his purse, take the right amount of money, and tie the meat around the dog's neck. Then the dog (5) ____ and (6) ____ . A regular customer was surprised to see the dog doing his shopping and (7) ____ follow him home. After about a mile, the dog approached a house and scratched at the door. When it opened, the customer said to the woman inside the house, "That's a very smart dog you have there." "Smart?" she replied. "Not really. That's the second time this week he's forgotten his front door keys."

2 [cassette] 74 Listen and check your answers to 1. Do you know any jokes or stories about animals? Tell your partner one of your jokes or stories.

Special Friends

Listening **1** [cassette] 75 Listen to Tim, Gus, and Maxine being interviewed about their pets. Guess what their pets are from the words in the box. Compare your guesses with a partner. The answers are on page B126.

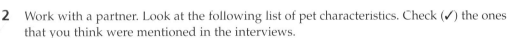

> a cat   a rat   a pig   a dog   a hamster   a parrot   a spider   a snake

2 Work with a partner. Look at the following list of pet characteristics. Check (✓) the ones that you think were mentioned in the interviews.

a) He's/She's a good companion.
b) He/She listens to my problems.
c) He/She makes me laugh when he/she does silly things.
d) We have a special bond.
e) He/She helps me make friends with other people with pets.
f) He/She scares people away.
g) He/She keeps me fit because I have to take him/her out for walks.
h) He/She looks cool.
i) He/She parties all night long.
j) He/She gives me unconditional love.

3 Listen to the interviews again and check your answers to 2. Put *T* for Tim, *G* for Gus, or *M* for Maxine if they mention that their pet has one of the characteristics.

4 Which of the characteristics in 2 would you look for in a pet? Which of these characteristics would you look for in a person? Discuss with a partner.

Tim

Gus

Maxine

Close-up

Conditionals

Yasmina would like to be a tiger.

1 Work with a partner. The diagram shows the last question from the interview in the previous section. Discuss the questions.

If-clause	Main clause
If + past tense *If you were an animal,*	*would* + simple verb form *what animal would you like to be?*

a) Is the question about a real situation or an unreal situation?
b) Is the question about now or the past? What tense is used in the *If*-clause?

2 Replace the word *animal* in the diagram in 1 with words from the box and/or your own ideas. Ask your partner the questions. Discuss your answers.

> a famous person   a fictional character   a color   a car   a month

3 Complete the *Unreal situation* column with conditional sentences so that they are true for you. Compare your sentences with your partner.

Real situation

a) I'm not a member of the opposite sex. → *If I were a member of the opposite sex,* *I'd/I wouldn't* ____ .

b) I'm not the president of my country. → If ____ , I'd/I wouldn't ____ .
c) I don't have $1 million. → If ____ , I'd/I wouldn't ____ .
d) I don't speak English fluently. → If ____ , I'd/I wouldn't ____ .
e) I can't fly a plane. → If ____ , I'd/I wouldn't ____ .

4 Work in small groups. Look at these "moral dilemmas." Complete them with the correct verb form and then discuss your answers to each one.

a) If you (**find**) a wallet in the street with $20, would you turn the wallet in to the police—but keep the cash?
b) If you saw your friend's partner kissing someone else, (**you tell**) your friend?
c) If a salesclerk (**give**) you too much change, would you keep the money and say nothing?
d) If a friend left his/her bag at your house by mistake, (**you look**) through it?
e) If you (**see**) some children stealing some chocolate from a store, would you tell the store owner?

5 Write down two more "moral dilemmas" beginning with *If* + past tense and pass them on to another group. Discuss the answers.

Language Reference: Conditionals

We can use a conditional sentence to talk about a present situation that is unreal or not probable. Conditional sentences have two clauses: an *If*-clause and a main clause.

If-clause
To show that a present situation is unreal, we use a past tense.

Main clause
We usually use *would* + simple verb form in the main clause.

Real situation	Unreal situation	If-clause	Main clause
time (now) = simple present →	time (now) = simple past	If I had $1 million,	I'd travel around the world.
I am not an animal. →	If I were/was an animal, ...*	If I could fly a plane,	I'd sell my car.
I live in an apartment. →	If I lived in an igloo, ...		

*Note: We use **were** with singular pronouns *I, he, she,* and *it* to emphasize that the situation is unreal. You will also sometimes hear **was** in informal spoken English.

Reptiles

Reading   **1**   Read the article about a pet snake and explain the links between the following.

a) 2 years old—5 years old   b) 6 inches—3 feet   c) 2 minutes—3 months

KING JIM

My son has been interested in having a snake as a pet since he was two. I think he's fascinated by their power to make people like me run away in horror. I've never been big on the idea of having a snake in the house, and I was hoping he would get tired of asking for one in the end, but his
5   stepfather went ahead and bought a little surprise snake for Louis's fifth birthday.

It was quite sweet: about six inches long and the width of a pencil— a non-venomous Californian King snake that Louis called King Jim. But then it grew and grew and grew. A year and a half later, it was about three feet long and as thick as a sausage. Some people objected to it so much that they
10   stopped coming to our house.

Personally, I disapprove of keeping a wild animal as a pet. It must get so bored with going around and around in its cage. I know he's unhappy, because once when Louis left the cage door open for a couple of minutes, King Jim escaped in a flash. We worried about him dying of cold or hunger, but to our
15   surprise, he showed up in the kitchen downstairs three months later.

When I think about it now, I can't believe we didn't tell our friends that we had an escaped snake in the house.

(Based on an article in the *Guardian Weekend*)

2   Would you have a pet snake? What's the most unusual pet you know? Tell your partner.

Vocabulary: prepositions after verbs and adjectives

1   Study the examples from the article above. Then complete the sentences to make some true and some false statements about yourself.

verb or adjective	preposition	*-ing* form or noun or pronoun
My son has been interested	*in*	*having a snake.* (line 1)
Some people objected	*to*	*it.* (line 9)

a)   At school, I was fascinated *by* ... (line 2)
b)   I've never been big _____ ... (line 3)
c)   As a child, I never got tired _____ ... (line 4)
d)   My parents disapprove _____ ... (line 11)

e)   I'll never get bored _____ ... (line 12)
f)   I often worry _____ ... (line 14)
g)   I feel happy when I think _____ ... (line 16)

2   Work with a partner. Read your partner's statements from 1 and guess which statements are true and which are false.

Anecdote   **1**   📼 76 Listen to Mandy talking about her friend's pet iguana. Which of the following topics does she talk about?

☐ What kind of animal is it?   ☐ What kind of personality does it have?

☐ Who is its owner?   ☐ Where does it sleep?

☐ What's its name?   ☐ What does it eat?

☐ How old is it?   ☐ Does it need much exercise?

☐ What does it look like?   ☐ Can it do any tricks?

2   Work with a partner. Write down as much information as you can remember about the topics Mandy talks about. Listen again and check your answers.

3   Think about a pet that you know: yours or somebody else's. You are going to tell your partner about it. Choose from the list in 1 the things you want to talk about. Think about what you will say and what language you will need.

Weird

Work in small groups. Look at the photograph below and discuss the questions.

- What do you know about crop circles?
- Who or what do you think made them?
- How do you think they are made?

> **crop circles** Patterns that began mysteriously appearing in fields in England and some other European countries in the 1980s.

Reading

Many theories have been suggested about who or what causes crop circles. Read this list of possible explanations and decide which is most and least believable. Discuss your answers with your partner.

THE CREAM OF THE

CROP CIRCLE
THEORIES

●

WIND Strong winds blow the corn into spiral patterns.

ALIENS The circles are landing sites for alien spacecraft or messages from other planets. People say they have seen bright flashing lights on the nights when crop circles have appeared.

MAGNETIC FORCES The crop circles are produced by magnetic forces under the earth.

WEAPONS TESTING The crop circles are caused by military tests that the army wants to keep secret.

HELICOPTERS The patterns are caused by the wind produced by helicopter rotor blades.

HOAXERS Groups of people create the crop circles at night. They say that they have made most, but not all, of the crop circles over the years.

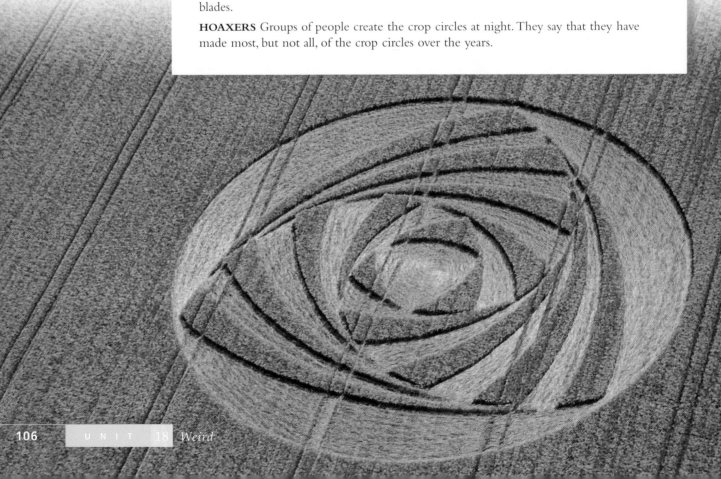

The Mother of All Circles

1 ⏺ 77 One night in August 2001, the crop circle in this photograph appeared in southern England. You are going to listen to a crop circle expert being interviewed about it. Listen and complete each question with the correct word.

a) How ____ have you been interested in crop circles?

b) How ____ is it exactly?

c) How ____ circles are there all together?

d) How ____ does it take to make a crop circle?

e) How ____ have crop circles existed?

Alton Barnes, Hampshire, England

2 Work with a partner. Match the questions in 1 to the answers below. Listen to the interview again and check your ideas.

1 About a half a mile wide.
2 Since 1980.
3 For about eleven years.

4 More than 400.
5 A few hours or several days.

3 What information in the interview did you find most surprising? How do *you* think the Alton Barnes crop circle was formed? Discuss with your partner.

Vocabulary:
***How* + adjective / adverb...?**

1 All of the questions in 1 above use the construction *How* + adjective/adverb. Make eight more questions by combining the question beginnings (*a–h*) with the most appropriate question ends (*1–8*). In some cases, more than one combination is possible.

a) How long
b) How often
c) How many
d) How much
e) How far
f) How fast
g) How old
h) How well

1 cousins do you have?
2 does your car go?
3 do you travel by train?
4 is the oldest living person in your family?
5 does it take you to get to work/school?
6 is it from your house to the nearest beach?
7 do you know your neighbors?
8 cash do you have on you right now?

2 Use the questions in 1 and your own ideas to interview your partner.

3 Complete the chart by writing down how long it takes you to do each activity. Guess the time it takes your partner to do the same things and then ask questions to check your ideas.

For example: *How long does it take you to get up in the morning?*

	Activity	You	Your partner
How long...?	• get up in the morning • eat lunch during a work day • buy presents for people you love • choose from a menu in a restaurant • decide whether you like someone or not • get ready to go out for the evening • get to sleep at night		

Incredible but True

1 You are going to read three true stories. In each case, a sentence is missing from the story. Match each of the sentences with a story and then reinsert the sentence in the appropriate position–1, 2, or 3.

a) She was now nearly 22 and hadn't met the love of her life yet.

b) At that time, Amy didn't know that Ian had just started a trip from Sydney to London.

c) It was a reply from another Laura Buxton, who had found the balloon in her backyard 140 miles away.

A Two Lauras

Laura Buxton, 10, was celebrating her grandparents' golden wedding anniversary when she had an idea. **1** She decided to release a gold and white helium-filled balloon with her name and address and a note attached. In the note, she asked the person who found the balloon to write back. Ten days later, a letter arrived at her home. **2** Both Lauras were 10 years old, and each has a three-year-old black Labrador, a guinea pig, and a rabbit. **3** "I talked to Laura on the phone," said the first Laura. "I hope we can become best friends. We have lots in common."

B Worlds Apart

Amy Dolby took her seat on the flight from London to Sydney, Australia. She was going to Australia to surprise her boyfriend, Ian Johnstone. **1** He wanted to propose to Amy on July 1 because this was the fifth anniversary of their relationship. **2** They both stopped in Singapore to wait for connecting flights, but they didn't know that they were sitting a few feet away from each other. **3** Ian arrived in Amy's hometown just as she knocked on his door in Sydney. When they found out what had happened, Ian proposed over the phone, and Amy accepted.

C Text Before Marriage

A clairvoyant had once told Emily Brown that she would meet her husband when she was 21. **1** One day, she tapped the text message, "Do you want to talk?" into her cell phone. She then invented a number and sent the message. She didn't know that the number belonged to her future husband. **2** Peter Baldwin was at work 140 miles away when he got the message. He called Emily, and they talked for about an hour. **3** They found that they had lots in common and made arrangements to meet. They got married six months later.

2 🔊 78 Listen and check your answers to 1.

3 Work in small groups. Discuss these questions.

• Have you ever read or heard about "incredible but true" stories like the stories in 1?

• Do you know any people (couples, friends, co-workers) who have met in a strange way?

• Have any strange coincidences or "small world" incidents ever happened to you?

1 Refer to the stories in the previous section and answer these questions.

a) Who <u>had an idea</u>?
b) Who <u>made arrangements</u> to meet someone?
c) Who <u>took her seat</u> on her flight to Australia?

2 Work with a partner. Look at the following statements and choose the appropriate verb in each case.

a) If you don't **have/make/take** risks, you won't succeed in life.
b) You should never **have/make/take** a promise if you can't keep it.
c) Everybody should **have/make/take** an experience of doing something dangerous once in their life.
d) All parents should **have/make/take** a course in parenting skills.
e) The press should not **have/make/take** photographs of famous people without their permission.
f) **Having/Making/Taking** mistakes is part of the process of learning a language.
g) The most important thing in life is to get a job where you can **have/make/take** lots of money.

3 Work with a partner. Decide if you agree or disagree with the statements in 2.

Close-up

1 Work with a partner. Look at the sentence from one of the stories in the previous section and discuss the following questions.

At that time, Amy <u>didn't know</u> that Ian <u>had just started</u> a trip from Sydney to London.

a) Both <u>underlined</u> verb structures describe past events. What is the name of each tense?
b) Which tense shows clearly that one past event happened before the other past event?
c) How do you form these tenses? Complete the chart.

	Affirmative	Negative	Question
Simple past	1 ___	She didn't know	2 ___ ?
Past perfect	He'd (had) started	3 ___	4 ___ ?

2 You are going to read two excerpts from a story titled *Reincarnation*. Read the first excerpt. Why did Jenny Cockell decide to travel to Ireland?

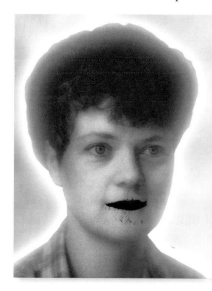

Reincarnation

Jenny Cockell was sure that she (1) **lived/had lived** before. As a child, she remembered her past life in her dreams. In particular, she often dreamed about Mary Sutton, a young Irish woman who (2) **died/had died** more than twenty years before Jenny was born. Over the years, Jenny became convinced that her dreams (3) **were/had been** real memories and that she (4) **was/had been** Mary in a previous life.

In her dreams, she saw the house in Ireland where Mary and her family (5) **lived/had lived**. As her visions continued and became more detailed, Jenny (6) **realized/had realized** that Mary (7) **died/had died** in 1930 and that her children could still be alive. She (8) **wanted/had wanted** to find out and decided to travel to Ireland.

3 ▪▪ 79 Work with a partner. Complete the first excerpt by choosing the most appropriate tense (simple past or past perfect) for each of the numbered verbs. Listen and check your answers.

4 Read the second excerpt. Who did Sonny think Jenny was? What do you think?

> In Ireland, Jenny quickly (1 **find**) the house that she (2 **see**) in her dreams. She then found out that Mary Sutton (3 **die**) in the early 1930s after giving birth to the last of eight children. After their mother's death, the children had all been sent to orphanages, but she finally contacted the eldest son, Sonny. It was an emotional day when Jenny (4 **meet**) the son she (5 **not see**) in fifty years. "I talked to him about our family life together. I (6 **remind**) him of the day when he (7 **catch**) a rabbit. There were lots of other memories, and they convinced him that I (8 **be**) his mother in a previous life."
>
> Jenny Cockell has written the story of her extraordinary past life experiences in a book titled *Yesterday's Children*.

5 🔲 80 Work with a partner. Complete the second excerpt by rewriting each of the numbered verbs in the most appropriate tense. Listen and check your answers.

6 Work with a partner. Discuss times you have felt some of the emotions in the box. Explain what had happened to make you feel that way.

When was the last time you	felt were	exhausted sad proud on top of the world frightened embarrassed jealous in a bad mood	?	What had happened? What had you done?

For example: *The last time I felt exhausted was on Friday. I'd been out till 3:00 A.M. ...*

Language Reference: Past perfect

We use the past perfect when we are talking about the past and we want to refer to an earlier past time. The past perfect clearly shows that one past event happened earlier than other past events.

As her visions **continued** and **became** more detailed, Jenny **realized** that Mary **had died** in 1930.

Earlier past	Past	Now

Anecdote

1 🔲 81 You are going to listen to Don and then Lidia talking about strange experiences they have had. Which of the following topics do they talk about?

Don and Lidia

Don Lidia

☐ ☐ Who had the strange experience? You, a member of your family, ...?

☐ ☐ Where was the person when it happened?

☐ ☐ Was the person alone?

☐ ☐ Did the person see or hear something strange?

☐ ☐ Did the person meet somebody in a strange situation?

☐ ☐ What exactly was strange about the experience?

☐ ☐ How did you or the person feel?

☐ ☐ What happened after the experience?

☐ ☐ What do you think about the experience? Can you explain it?

2 Work with a partner. Write down as much information as you can remember about each story. Listen again and check your answers. Which story do you think is stranger?

3 Think of a strange experience you or somebody you know has had. You are going to tell a partner about it. Choose from the list in 1 the things you want to talk about. Think about what you will say and what language you will need.

We Are Not Alone

1 You are going to read a short account of a famous UFO incident—a mysterious crash in Roswell, New Mexico, in 1947. How many different explanations are there for the crash? Do you believe any of the explanations?

Roswell, New Mexico

On July 8, 1947, the U.S. Air Force told the public that a flying saucer had crashed in Roswell, New Mexico, and that they had found bodies of aliens. Later the same day, the U.S. Air Force changed their story and told reporters that the flying saucer was in fact a weather balloon.

The story became famous when people said that the government had covered up the real story. Thirty years later, witnesses told newspapers that they had seen the aliens. They described the aliens in detail, and models were made according to their descriptions.

In 1994, the U.S. Air Force changed the story again. Now they said that the crash at Roswell in 1947 had been a top secret radar balloon used for spying on the USSR. When government officials investigated, they found that all documents recorded at Roswell from 1945 to 1949 had been destroyed more than forty years ago.

2 Work in small groups. Discuss these questions.

- Do you think there are forms of life on other planets?
- Do you think aliens have visited the Earth?
- What do you think aliens might look like?
- If you saw a UFO, what would you do?
- If you met an alien, what would you ask?
- If you had to elect someone to meet the alien leader, who would you choose? Why?
- If you could travel in a time machine, would you choose to go forward or backward in time? Why?

Writing **1** Work with a partner. Discuss ways of completing *The Night I Met an Alien* by answering the questions. Take notes and add as much detail as possible.

2 Write your story from the notes you took in 1. Compare your stories with other people in the class.

THE NIGHT I MET AN ALIEN

It was an ordinary evening.
What time was it?
What was the weather like?
What were you doing?

For some reason, I looked up at the sky, and I saw a strange object.
What did the object look like?

To my surprise, it landed, and an alien got out.
What did the alien look like?
How did you feel?

Then it spoke to me in perfect English.
What did it say?
What was its voice like?

I asked it what I'd always wanted to ask an alien.
What did you ask?

It answered my question.
What did it say?

Eventually, it got back in the object and flew away. I stood still for a while, and when I turned around, I noticed that something had changed.
What had changed?

My life would never be the same again.

19 *Wheels*

Reading

1 You are going to read three descriptions of people's first cars. Match each description (*A–C*) with one of the pictures (*1–3*) below. Which car caused its owner the most problems?

MY FIRST CAR

A My first car was a Ford Maverick. I think someone gave it to me—it was a real clunker. It used to break down almost every time I went out in it.

Once I was driving along a country road and the hood blew up against the windshield and blocked my view of the road. It was really dangerous because I couldn't see anything.

Another time, it was raining heavily, and one of the windshield wipers fell off. I had to stop and wait for the rain to stop.

I used to have a love/hate relationship with that car—I loved it when it worked, but I hated it when it broke down.

B It wasn't my car; it was my boyfriend's. It was a blue VW Beetle with a sunroof and whitewall tires.

Every weekend we used to drive to the country with our tent in the back and drive until we felt like stopping. Sometimes we took friends.

It wasn't a big car, but I remember one weekend we went to Montreal with four friends. There were six of us in this little car! I don't think we took any luggage, because there wasn't any space for suitcases. The engine was in the back, and there was only a tiny trunk in the front. But we didn't use to worry about that kind of thing when we were younger.

C Daddy gave me my first car when I was 17. I didn't even have my driver's license. It was a sweet little red Ferrari with a wooden steering wheel and black seats. It was cute, but I didn't use it much, because I used to prefer motorcycles. All my boyfriends had big motorcycles. My daddy used to introduce me to all these nice guys—lawyers and businessmen—but I wasn't interested in them. I was a rebel, and I used to enjoy the danger of going on fast motorcycles.

My poor daddy—I used to drive him crazy.

2 What was the first car you drove? Or what was the first car you remember going in as a child? Describe it to your partner.

Vocabulary: cars

1 Find nine words and expressions in the text in the previous section that describe parts of a car.

2 Work in small groups. Imagine you are going to buy a new car. Divide the following features into "important" and "not important." What other features are important in a car?

> air bags   air conditioning   easy to park   economical to run   electric sunroof
> good stereo   large trunk   leather seats   nice appearance   power steering
> powerful engine   radial tires   spacious interior

Anecdote   Imagine your dream car. You are going to tell your partner about it. Choose from the list below the things you want to talk about. Think about what you are going to say and how you are going to say it.

☐ What kind of car is it?

☐ Is it a modern car, or is it an old model?

☐ What color is it?

☐ What's it like inside?

☐ What kind of seats does it have?

☐ What special features does it have?

☐ What's the top speed?

☐ What CDs do you have in your car?

☐ Where would you like to go in your car?

☐ Who would you take with you?

Close-up

Past time: *used to* + simple verb form

Language Reference p. 114

1 Work with a partner. Look at these excerpts from the article in the previous section. Match each underlined verb structure with a description (1–3). In which case is it *not* possible to use *used to* + simple verb form to talk about the past?

a) "Every weekend we <u>used to drive</u> to the country…"   1 A single action in the past
b) "…one weekend we <u>went</u> to Montreal…"   2 A repeated action in the past
c) "I <u>used to have</u> a love/hate relationship with that car…"   3 A state in the past

2 Work with a partner. Look at the following sentences. Where it is possible, replace the simple past with *used to/didn't use to* + simple verb form.

When I was a child…
a) My parents <u>had</u> a big old Buick. *My parents used to have a big old Buick.*
b) My mother <u>drove</u> me to school every day.
c) I <u>didn't like</u> going on long car trips. I <u>got</u> car sick.
d) One summer we <u>went</u> to Canada on a camping trip.
e) My parents <u>never cleaned</u> the car. It <u>smelled</u> awful.
f) Eventually my parents <u>sold</u> the car and <u>bought</u> a smaller one.

3 Change the sentences in 2 so that they are true for you. Compare with a partner.

4 Work with a partner. Use the topics in the box and your own ideas to talk about and compare your life now with your life ten years ago.

> the vacations you go on   the car you have   the people you go out with
> the TV programs you watch   the amount of sleep you get   the hairstyle you have
> the things you do on weekends   the music you listen to

For example: *I used to spend every summer vacation at my grandparents' house at the shore. These days I usually go abroad. I love traveling…*

Language Reference: *Used to*

We can use *used to* + simple verb form to talk about past habits (repeated actions in the past) or past states. It describes things that were true in the past but are not true now.
*Every weekend **we used to drive** to the country.*
***We didn't use to worry** about that kind of thing.*
*What kind of car **did you use to have**?*

For and against Cars

1 Work in small groups. Discuss the advantages and disadvantages of owning a car. Write down as many points as you can.

2 [cassette] **82** You are going to listen to three friends discussing the same thing. Listen to their conversation. How many of the points you wrote down in 1 do they mention?

3 Work with a partner. Complete the conversation between Karen, Ron, and Jill with one word in each space. Then listen and check your answers.

K: You're late!

R: Yes, I'm really sorry—I had to wait forever for a bus.

J: Why didn't you drive?

R: Ah, well. I sold my car.

K: Oh, are you getting a new one?

R: No, I'm not getting another car. I've decided to live without one.

J: Wow—what made you do that?

R: I (1) *think* there are too many cars, and this city is far too polluted.

J: Well, that's true, (2) ____ a car is useful.

R: I don't think (3) ____ . Not in the city, anyway. I can never find anywhere to park, and you spend most of the time sitting in traffic jams.

K: But how are you going to get to work?

R: By bicycle.

K: (4) ____ you think bicycles are dangerous?

R: Not really. I don't think they're as dangerous as cars.

J: Well, I couldn't do without my car. I have to take the kids to school every day.

R: I don't (5) ____ children get enough exercise these days —they should walk to school.

K: Well, I don't have children, but I (6) ____ with Jill—I couldn't live without my car. I sometimes have to come home late from the office.

R: Why don't you take the bus? Public transportation is very good.

K: That's not (7) ____ . The buses are not very regular where I work, and anyway, as a woman, I don't feel safe waiting for a bus late at night.

R: O.K., I see what you (8) ____ , but aren't you worried about pollution?

J: Of course, but you don't understand—it's easy for you to worry about the environment. I have to worry about carrying the groceries and kids and . . .

R: O.K., O.K., you're (9) ____ ! Come on. Let's change the subject. Hey, (10) ____ do you think of my new haircut?

4 [cassette] **83** Listen and repeat the highlighted expressions. Copy the stress and intonation exactly.

5 Whose opinion do you agree with most?

Close-up

Opinions

1 Look at the highlighted text in the conversation in the previous section. Find another expression to show each of the following functions.

    a)   Ask for an opinion: (1) *Don't you think…* (2) ____
    b)   Give an opinion: (1) *I think…* (2) ____
    c)   Agree partly with an opinion: (1) *Well, that's true, but…* (2) ____
    d)   Agree completely with an opinion: (1) *I agree with…* (2) ____
    e)   Disagree with an opinion: (1) *I don't think so.* (2) ____

2 Work in groups of three. Complete the following task.

    a)   Choose one of the topics in the box (or your own idea) and write down all the advantages and disadvantages that you can think of.
    b)   Write a short conversation between three friends with your ideas from *a*. Use expressions from 1.
    c)   Act out your conversation in front of the class. Vote for the best conversation.

> fast food   living abroad   being a woman or a man   being rich or famous
> public transportation   marriage   cloning   capital punishment
> living with your parents   private education

Advice and suggestions

1 🔲 84 You are going to listen to a radio talk show called *Road Rage*. Listeners call the radio station with travel questions and problems, and the host, Dave Pearl, gives them advice. Listen and check (✓) which of the following problems are mentioned.

    a)   I want to go somewhere nice on vacation, but I hate flying.
    b)   I'm sick of wasting time in traffic jams.
    c)   I'm a bus driver, and I don't get enough exercise.
    d)   My husband, who is usually kind and considerate, gets very aggressive when he is driving. It frightens me.
    e)   I can drive, but I can't pass my test.
    f)   I don't want to contribute to the pollution of the environment.

2 Work with a partner. Dave gives Mark three pieces of advice. Listen again and match the beginnings with the ends of each sentence. Do you think this is good advice?

    a)   Why don't you…   1   use public transportation.
    b)   You could…   2   learn a new language.
    c)   If I were you, I'd…   3   work at home?

3 Work with a partner. If you were Dave Pearl, what advice would you give to the second caller, Sharon? Use the sentence beginnings in 2 and make some suggestions.

4 Work with a partner. Invent and act out short conversations where Student A has a problem and Student B gives some advice. Use the other travel problems in 1 or your own ideas as your starting point.

Language Reference: Opinions, advice, and suggestions

There are many ways to ask for, give, agree with, or disagree with opinions.

Ask for an opinion: ***What do you think of*** my new jacket?
Give an opinion: ***I think*** it's great.   ***I don't think*** it's very nice.
Agree with an opinion: Partly: ***That's true, but… I see what you mean, but…***
                       Completely: ***I agree with you. You're right.***
Disagree with an opinion: ***I don't think so. That's not true.***

There are many ways of giving advice or making suggestions.

Why don't you work at home? ***You could*** use public transportation.
If I were you, I'd learn a new language.

A Family Vacation

Reading and listening

Bill Bryson

Bill Bryson was born in the United States but lived for many years in England. He's the best-selling author of many humorous travel books.

1 ▶ 85 Read and listen to this excerpt from a book called *The Lost Continent*, by Bill Bryson. He is describing the vacation trips he used to take with his family. Is each of the following statements true or false? Compare your answers with a partner.

a) The writer used to go on vacation with his parents and his cousins.
b) The children used to make a "bomb" that looked like a porcupine.
c) The "bombs" used to make other cars crash.
d) The parents never used to understand why other drivers got angry.
e) Most of the time, the mother used to keep quiet.

In my memory, our vacations were always taken in a big blue Rambler station wagon. It was a cruddy car—my dad always bought cruddy cars, until he got to the male menopause and started buying zippy red
5 convertibles—but it had space. My brother, sister, and I in the back were miles away from my parents up front. We <u>quickly</u> discovered that if you stuck matches into an apple or hard-boiled egg so that it resembled a porcupine and <u>casually</u> dropped it out the window, it was like a bomb. It would
10 explode with a small bang and a surprisingly big flash of blue flame, causing cars following behind to veer in an amusing fashion.

My dad, miles away up front, never knew what was going on and could not understand why all day long cars would zoom up alongside him, with the driver gesticulating <u>furiously</u> before tearing off into the distance. "What was that all
15 about?" he would say to my mother.

"I don't know, dear," my mother would answer <u>mildly</u>. My mother only ever said two things. She said, "I don't know, dear." And she said, "Can I get you a sandwich, honey?"

Occasionally on our trips she would volunteer other pieces of intelligence
20 like, "I think you hit that dog/man/blind person back there, honey," but mostly she <u>wisely</u> kept quiet.

(From The Lost Continent, by Bill Bryson)

2 Match adverbs <u>underlined</u> in the text in 1 with adverbs from the box below to get pairs with similar meanings.

angrily   in a relaxed way   intelligently   gently   rapidly

3 Find the following words in the text and choose the most appropriate meaning from the alternatives.

a) a station wagon (line 2): (1) *a big car with a long body*; (2) *a small sports car*
b) cruddy (line 2): (1) *lovely and new*; (2) *old and ugly*
c) zippy (line 4): (1) *fast*; (2) *slow*
d) to veer (line 11): (1) *to continue driving in a straight line*; (2) *to change direction suddenly*
e) zoom up (line 13): (1) *drive slowly*; (2) *drive fast*
f) tearing off (line 14): (1) *driving away fast*; (2) *driving away slowly*

4 What did you use to do to pass the time on long car trips when you were a child? Tell your partner.

24 Hours from Tulsa

Song

1 Work with a partner. The pictures illustrate a song called *24 Hours from Tulsa*. Discuss which is the most logical order for the story.

2 ⬛ 86 Listen and read the lyrics of the song and check your ideas in 1.

Dearest Darling,
I had to write to say that I won't be home anymore.
'Cause something happened to me,
While I was driving (1) ____ and I'm not the same
    anymore.

Oh, I was only twenty-four hours from Tulsa,
Ah, only one day away from your arms,
I saw a welcoming (2) ____ ,
And stopped to rest for the night.

And that is when I saw her,
As I pulled (3) ____ outside of the small hotel
    she was there.
And so I walked up to her,
Asked where I could get (4) ____ to eat and
    she showed me where.

Oh, I was only twenty-four hours from Tulsa,
Ah, only one day away from your arms.
She took me to the cafe.
I asked her if she would stay.
She said okay.

Oh, I was only twenty-four hours from Tulsa,
Ah, only one day away from your arms.
The jukebox started to play
And nighttime (5) ____ into day.

As we were dancing (6) ____ ,
All of a sudden I lost (7) ____ as I held her charms.
And I caressed her, kissed her,
Told her I'd die before I would let her out of my arms.

Oh, I was only twenty-four hours from Tulsa,
Ah, only one day away from your arms.
I hate to do (8) ____ to you,
But I love somebody new.
What can I do?

And I can never, never, never
Go home again.

3 Complete the lyrics with words from the box. Listen again and check your answers.

*24 Hours
from Tulsa*

This was a big hit for
Gene Pitney in 1963.
Gene Pitney has been
a star for over thirty
years.

closely	control	home	in	light	something	this	turned

4 The song is the story of why a man has decided to break up with his partner. Work in small groups. Discuss these questions.

a) What do you think of the man in the song?
b) What do you think of the woman at the hotel in the song?
c) What do you think is the kindest or cruelest way to break up with a partner?

Review 4

Big Game Lottery

Language reviewed: past time—*used to* (Unit 19); prepositions after verbs and adjectives (Unit 17); *will* for prediction (Unit 16); future time clauses (Unit 16); conditionals (Unit 17)

Work with a partner. Look at the proverbs below. Do you have similar proverbs in your language? Which of these proverbs do you agree with?

"The best things in life are free."
"Money is the root of all evil."
"If something can go wrong, it will go wrong."

Reading   **1**   Read the newspaper article about a lottery winner. If you were in Mrs. Alvarado's position, would you feel the same as her? Why/Why not?

Colorado Woman Wins Top Prize

A 67-year-old woman has won $198 million in the Big Game Lottery, the biggest prize in U.S. history. Eva Alvarado, who **moved** to the United States in 1984, lives in Colorado Springs, where she works as a cleaner in a home for mentally handicapped children.

Two years ago, Mrs. Alvarado's husband **died** in an accident in the potato factory in Bingham County, Idaho, where they both **worked**. "We **hated** that factory, and we **played** the lottery every week because we **dreamed** of escaping to a better life," Mrs. Alvarado **said** yesterday. "But when Ramón died, I moved here, and I don't want to change my life now. This job is the luckiest thing that has ever happened to me. I don't want to leave the children."

Mrs. Alvarado **told** reporters that she wanted to spend some of the money on a new playroom for the children's home.

2   Work with a partner. Read the article again. Which four verbs in **bold** can you replace with the structure *used to* + simple verb form? Why can't you replace the other verbs with the same structure?

Past time: **1**   Look at the following statements. Where possible, replace the simple past verb forms
used to   with *used to* or *didn't use to*.

a)   I was born in a hospital.
b)   As a child, I lived in a small town.
c)   I shared a bedroom with my brother/sister.
d)   I watched the Cartoon Network on TV every day.
e)   My parents gave me lots of pocket money.
f)   We went to Disneyland once as a special treat.
g)   I didn't enjoy English classes at school.

2   How many of the statements in 1 were true for you as a child? Rewrite the sentences so that they are all true for you. Compare your sentences with a partner.

Listening

1 ◼◼ **87** You are going to listen to a radio talk show where callers comment on Mrs Alvarado's lottery win. Complete each of these comments with an appropriate preposition. Listen and check your answers.

a) Mrs. Alvarado is obviously very fond ____ the children.
b) She will soon get tired ____ all the letters.
c) She needs to think ____ her future now.
d) She doesn't sound very excited ____ winning the lottery.
e) She's more interested ____ the children than the money.
f) She doesn't have to worry ____ the future anymore.

2 Look at some predictions about Mrs. Alvarado's life. Listen again and check (✓) the ones you heard on the radio program.

a) She'll quit her job soon.
b) Life will be very difficult.
c) Everyone will ask her for money.
d) She'll buy a new house and a car.
e) She'll give most of the money away.
f) She'll need a financial advisor.
g) She'll take a long vacation.
h) She'll change her mind about giving money to the children's home.

3 Work with a partner. Which of the predictions in 2 would you make? Do you think it is possible to continue the same lifestyle if you win the lottery? What would you do if you won $198 million?

Future time clauses

1 Complete each sentence with the correct alternative.

a) As soon as the class **'ll end/ends**, Becky's going to buy a lottery ticket.
b) Terry will get married when he **'ll meet/meets** the right girl.
c) As soon as Ron **'ll get/gets** home tonight, he's going to do his homework.
d) If it **'ll rain/rains** tomorrow, Jenny will probably come in by car.
e) Sandy will probably retire when she **'ll be/is** fifty.
f) Tim will probably get a well-paying job when he **'ll finish/finishes** college.

2 Work with a partner. Replace the names in 1 with names of people in the class. How many true statements can you make?

Conditionals

1 Change the following "facts" if necessary to make them all true for you. Then write conditional "dream" sentences. Compare your sentences with your partner.

Facts	Dreams
a) I don't have $1 million.	➜ *If I... If I had $1 million, I'd buy a beautiful yacht.*
b) I don't speak perfect English.	➜ *If I...*
c) I'm not the mayor of this city.	➜ *If I...*
d) I can't travel in time.	➜ *If I...*
e) I'm a man/woman.	➜ *If I...*

2 Work with a partner. Choose a conditional sentence from 1 and take turns adding to a chain of conditions. Who can create the longest "conditional chain"?

For example:

STUDENT A

If I had $1 million, I'd buy a beautiful yacht.

STUDENT B

If I bought a beautiful yacht, I'd sail around the Caribbean.

If I sailed around the Caribbean, I'd ... etc.

It's Your Lucky Day!

Language reviewed: relative clauses and relative pronouns (Unit 17); *have/make/take* + noun structures (Unit 18); *how* + adjective/adverb (Unit 18); past perfect (Unit 18)

Relative clauses

1 Complete each question by choosing the correct alternative.

a) Do you know anyone who **is/he is** really lucky or unlucky?

b) Are there any numbers that **are/they are** especially lucky for you?

c) Do you wear or carry an object that **brings/it brings** you luck?

d) Is there anything special that **do/you do** before an exam to bring you luck?

e) Have you ever received a letter or an e-mail that **promised/it promised** you good luck?

2 Work with a partner. Discuss the questions in 1.

Reading

1 If you received this e-mail message, what would you do? Discuss with a partner.

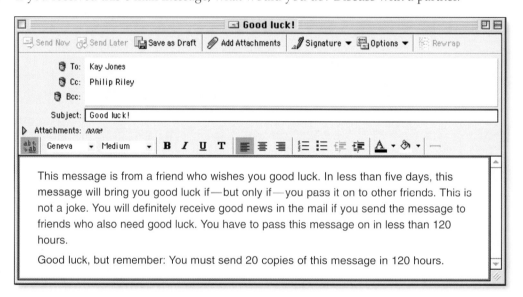

2 The e-mail continues below with stories about people who did or didn't pass on the e-mail message. Complete the text by choosing the appropriate verb.

- Ana Cuevas from Peru was (1) **making/taking** a course in Web programming. She (2) **made/took** her final exam two days after receiving the message and got an excellent grade.

- A New York stockbroker received the message on her first day at a new job. The next week, she (3) **had/made** $14 million for her company.

- An 83-year-old, Piotr Wojdylo, (4) **had/took** a serious illness, and the doctors said he (5) **had/took** only six months to live. He was (6) **making/taking** arrangements for his funeral when he got the message. Five years later, he is alive and well.

- A businessman from Salt Lake City received the message but (7) **had/made** the mistake of asking his secretary to pass it on. She forgot. Four days later, he (8) **had/took** a terrible car accident, even though he was driving at only 15 mph.

- Photographer Wesley Pratt waited outside Madonna's home for six days. Finally, he (9) **made/took** the pictures that he wanted, but when the film was developed, the pictures were black. He had completely forgotten to pass on the message.

- Regina Witte received good luck messages every Monday for three months but did nothing. Finally, she decided to (10) **make/take** the risk of deleting the message from her computer. She (11) **had/made** the wrong decision! Her computer crashed one hour later.

3 Work with a partner. Complete each question with a word from the box.

fast	long	long	much	often	old	well

a) How ____ did Ana Cuevas do on her examination?
b) How ____ money did the New York stockbroker make?
c) How ____ was the man with the serious illness?
d) How ____ did the doctors say he would live?
e) How ____ was the businessman from Salt Lake City driving?
f) How ____ did the photographer wait to take pictures of Madonna?
g) How ____ did Regina Witte receive good luck messages?

4 Read the e-mail message in 2 again and answer the questions in 3.

Past perfect **1** Read the article below and explain the title.

A Lucky **Escape**

The day started badly. I woke up late because I (1 **forget**) about the alarm clock the night before. I got dressed in five minutes and called a taxi to take me to the airport. Thirty minutes later, the taxi still hadn't arrived. I called the taxi company, and they explained that the taxi (2 **break down**). So I decided to take my own car to JFK, picked up my bag, and left the house. But when I got in the car, the engine wouldn't start. I realized that I (3 **leave**) the headlights on the night before. I decided to try the taxi company again, but when I put my hand in my pocket, my telephone wasn't there. I (4 **leave**) it in the kitchen, so I went back inside to get it. I opened the door and could hear the radio, which I (5 **forget**) to turn off. "This is the eight o'clock news on WNBV. It's Sunday, April seventh," I heard. "Eight o'clock," I thought. "But it's only seven o'clock," and I looked at my watch to check. Suddenly, I remembered. It *was* eight o'clock! The clocks (6 **change**) that weekend! There was no point going to the airport now. The plane (7 **already take off**). But as I sat there listening to the news, I realized how lucky I had been. The plane (8 **crash**) just after take-off at JFK, and it was feared that all 217 people aboard (9 **die**).

This is the eight o'clock News on WNBV.

2 Work with a partner. Complete the story by putting the verbs into the past perfect.

3 88 Listen and check your answers.

Anecdote Think about a lucky or unlucky experience you have had. You are going to tell your partner about it. Choose from the list below the things you want to talk about. Think about what you will say and what language you will need.

☐ Was it a lucky or unlucky experience?
☐ When did it happen?
☐ Where were you?
☐ Who were you with?

☐ What were you doing?
☐ What happened?
☐ Why was it lucky (or unlucky)?
☐ How did you feel afterward?

Let's Talk About ...

START

1 ...somebody with an unusual name

2 ...somebody who is important to you

27 ...the person you talk to most on the phone

28 ...the most helpful person you know

29 ...a time you were late

30 ...the healthiest person you know

26 ...a foreign person you know

25 ...the last time you went out and had a good time

24 ...your favorite historical figure

FINISH

38 ...three good reasons for learning English

23 ...a time when you got into trouble

22 ...something you feel strongly about

21 ...how you relax

20 ...things that make you happy or unhappy

19 ...your favorite subject in school

18 ...the qualities of your ideal partner

3
...your favorite city

4
...a place you don't like

5
...your dream vacation

6
...a couple you know

7
...a romantic movie

31
...the kind of food you love or hate

32
...a pet you know

8
...how you keep fit

33
...the kind of people you don't like

9
...playing sports at school

34
...the slowest person you know

10
...an interesting character in a movie

35
...a strange experience

11
...one of your neighbors

37
...a terrible journey

36
...your dream car

12
...the best present you've ever received

13
...the last present you bought someone

17
...your plans for next weekend

16
...a pop band you love or hate

15
...a retired person you know

14
...the best or worst job you can imagine

Play the game in small groups. You will need a die and counters.

1 Place your counters on the square marked START and throw the die.

2 The first player to throw a six starts the game.

3 The first player throws the die and moves his/her counter along the board according to the number on the die.

4 Players then take turns moving around the board.

5 When a player lands on a blue square, he/she has to talk about the subject for thirty seconds.

6 When players land on an orange square, they have to talk about the subject for sixty seconds.

7 If a player has nothing to say or can't talk for the necessary time, he/she is allowed to pass and miss a turn.

8 The game continues until the first player reaches the square marked FINISH.

Additional material

11 Smile

Vocabulary: the face, 5

11 Smile

Vocabulary: describing character, 4

Your description of a dog is your own personality.

Your description of a cat is your partner's personality.

Your description of a rat is your enemy's personality.

Your description of coffee is how you see love.

Your description of an ocean is your own life.

11 Smile

What Are You Like?
Reading, 1

If you scored 19–24,
YOU'RE AN OPTIMIST!
You always try to see the positive side of life. You know how to enjoy yourself, and you don't waste time worrying about things that may never happen. But be careful—your friends might find your optimism rather irritating at times.

If you scored 13–18,
YOU'RE MR. OR MS. SENSIBLE!
You are a realist. You know life has ups and downs, but you hope to have more good times than bad times in your life. But be careful— you can be too serious at times. You need to show your feelings a little more.

If you scored 8–12,
YOU'RE A PESSIMIST!
You should try to stop having negative thoughts. You need to learn how to enjoy the good things in life and stop worrying about things that may never happen. And remember, there are many people in worse situations than you.

13 Dance

Reading

What it means

If you scored 20–29
When you dance, you really express yourself. You may look like an octopus in a blender, but you don't care what other people think. Good for you! No party is complete without you.

If you scored 11–19
You enjoy dancing, but you're too worried about your image. You should let yourself go. Be a little less serious about life.

If you scored 10 or less
Hmm, what *do* you enjoy? Do you collect stamps? Hopefully you are an interesting person to talk to!

15 Review 3

National Sports. Dynamic and stative meanings, 2
Student A

17 Animals

Vocabulary: animals
Answers:
a 4   b 3   c 5   d 1   e 6   f 2

16 Lifestyle

Close-up. *will* for prediction, 2

The Oracle

- Choose a question you want to ask.
- Take turns rolling the die, keeping the question in your mind.
- Find the letter corresponding to your question and the number you threw on the die. Find your answer where they meet. For example, you asked question *d* and you threw *4*, so the Oracle says, "One of each."

a) What will the love of my life look like?
b) Will I be famous one day?
c) Will I travel the world?
d) How many children will I have?
e) Where will I be the happiest?
f) What will I look like in ten years?

15 Review 3

National Sports. Passives, 1

a) False—Barcelona.
b) False—eleven players.
c) True.
d) True.
e) False—but it wasn't broken till 1991 (twenty-three years later). His jump at the Mexico City Olympics is considered by many to be the greatest athletic achievement of all time.
f) False—Germany was beaten by Brazil 2–0.

	1	2	3	4	5	6
a	Not as you expect.	Gorgeous.	Not classically good-looking, but you'll never look at anybody else.	Very fit.	He/She will have wonderful eyes.	He/She'll look like you.
b	No, you won't.	No, but you'll meet someone famous.	You'll be well-known in your profession.	You'll be in the news for doing something crazy.	You'll have your fifteen minutes of fame.	Yes, but you'll have to work very hard.
c	Yes, for pleasure.	Yes, for your job.	No, but you'll travel in your own country.	No, but you'll meet people from all over the world.	You'll have wonderful vacations abroad.	You'll travel when you're older.
d	More than you expect.	The same as your parents.	Your career will be more important.	One of each.	You'll have a big family.	Enough.
e	At home in bed.	In the mountains.	Abroad.	Near the ocean.	Everywhere.	In a big city.
f	Completely different.	Like your mother.	Fabulous.	Younger than you are.	No different.	Like your father.

15 Review 3

National Sports. Stative and dynamic meanings, 2
Student B

17 Animals

Special Friends. Listening, 1

Tim's pig, Harriet   Gus's spider, Hendrix   Maxine's hamster, Page

Verb structures

Basic structures

| ASPECT | VOICE | TENSES | |
		Present	Past
simple	active	He **writes** letters.	He **wrote** letters.
	passive	Letters **are written**.	Letters **were written**.
continuous	active	He **is writing** letters.	He **was writing** letters.
	passive	Letters **are being written**.	Letters **were being written**.
perfect	active	He **has written** letters.	He **had written** letters.
	passive	Letters **have been written**.	Letters **had been** written.
perfect continuous	active	He **has been writing** letters.	He **had been writing** letters.

Simple present
See Unit 12.

Affirmative	Negative	Question
I/You/We/They **write**.	I/You/We/They **don´t (do not) write**.	**Do** I/you/we/they **write**?
He/She/It **writes**.	He/She/It **doesn´t (does not) write**.	**Does** he/she/it **write**?

Present continuous
See Unit 12.

Affirmative	Negative	Question
I'm (am) **writing**.	I'm not (am not) **writing**.	**Am** I **writing**?
You/We/They're (are) **writing**.	You/We/They're not (are not) **writing**.	**Are** you/we/they **writing**?
He/She/It's (is) **writing**.	He/She/It **isn't** (is not) **writing**.	**Is** he/she/it **writing**?

Note: When a verb ends with a single vowel letter followed by a single consonant letter, we usually double the final consonant letter before *-ing*: *chat – chatting; jog – jogging; refer – referring; stop – stopping.*

Present perfect
See Unit 13.

Affirmative	Negative	Question
I/You/We/They 've (have) **written**.	I/You/We/They **haven't** (have not) **written**.	**Have** I/you/we/they **written**?
He/She/It's (has) **written**.	He/She/It **hasn't** (has not) **written**.	**Has** he/she/it **written**?

Note: See list of irregular verbs on page B130.

Present perfect continuous
See Unit 13.

Affirmative	Negative	Question
I/You/We/They 've (have) been **writing**.	I/You/We/They **haven't** (have not) been **writing**.	**Have** I/you/we/they been **writing**?
He/She/It's (has) been **writing**.	He/She/It **hasn't** (has not) been **writing**.	**Has** he/she/it been **writing**?

Simple past

Affirmative	Negative	Question
I/You/He/She/ It/We/They **wrote**.	I/You/He/She/ It/We/They **didn't (did not) write**.	**Did** I/you/he/she/it/we/they **write**?

Note: See list of irregular verbs on page B130. When a verb ends with a single vowel letter followed by a single consonant letter, we usually double the final consonant letter before *-ed*: *chat – chatted; jog – jogged; refer – referred; stop – stopped.*

Past continuous

Affirmative	Negative	Question
I/He/She/It **was writing**.	I/He/She/It **wasn't (was not) writing**.	**Was** I/He/She/It **writing**?
You/We/They **were writing**.	You/We/They **weren't (were not) writing**.	**Were** you/we/they **writing**?

Past perfect
See Unit 18.

Affirmative	Negative	Question
I/You/He/She/ It/We/They 'd (had) **written**.	I/You/He/She/ It/We/They **hadn't** (had not) **written**.	**Had** I/you/he/she/it/we/they **written**?

Note: See list of irregular verbs on page B130.

used to
See Unit 19.

Affirmative	Negative	Question
I/You/He/She/ It/We/They **used to write**.	I/You/He/She/ It/We/They **didn't** use to write.	**Did** I/you/he/she/it/we/they **use to write**?

(be) going to

Affirmative	Negative	Question
I'm (am) going to write.	I'm not (am not) going to write.	Am I going to write?
You/We/They're (are) going to write.	You/We/They're not (are not) going to write.	Are you/we/they going to write?
He/She/It's (is) going to write.	He/She/It isn't (is not) going to write.	Is he/she/it going to write?

Present continuous for future

See page B127 (Present continuous).

will

See Unit 16.

Affirmative	Negative	Question
I/You/He/She/It/We/They'll (will) write.	I/You/He/She/It/We/They won't (will not) write.	Will I/You/He/She/It/We/They write?

Modals

Affirmative	Negative	Question
can: see Unit 14.		
I/You/He *etc.* can write.	I/You/He *etc.* can't (cannot) write.	Can I/you/he *etc.* write?
could: see Unit 14.		
I/You/He *etc.* could write.	I/You/He *etc.* couldn't (could not) write.	Could I/you/he *etc.* write?
must		
I/You/He *etc.* must write.	I/You/He *etc.* mustn't (must not) write.	Must I/you/he *etc.* write?
may		
I/You/He *etc.* may write.	I/You/He *etc.* may not write.	May I/you/he *etc.* write?
might		
I/You/He *etc.* might write.	I/You/He *etc.* mightn't (might not) write.	Might I/you/he *etc.* write?
should: see Unit 19.		
I/You/He *etc.* should write.	I/You/He *etc.* shouldn't (should not) write.	Should I/you/he *etc.* write?
will: see Unit 16.		
I/You/He *etc.* 'll (will) write.	I/You/He *etc.* won't (will not) write.	Will I/you/he, *etc.* write?
would: see Unit 17.		
I/You/He *etc.* 'd (would) write.	I/You/He *etc.* wouldn't (would not) write.	Would I/you/he *etc.* write?

Future time clauses

See Unit 16.

Subordinate clause	Main clause
If he has a cigarette,	he'll be in big trouble.
When he finishes the week,	he'll feel like a new man.
As soon as he arrives,	he'll take a fitness test.

Note: The two clauses can usually be used in either order; for example:
He'll be in big trouble if he has a cigarette.

Conditional clauses

See Unit 17.

If-clause	Main clause
If I had $1 million,	I'd travel around the world. I'd buy a big house.
If I were* an animal,	I'd be a lion. I'd be a bird so I could fly.
If I could live anywhere,	I'd choose somewhere hot. I wouldn't stay here!

*You will sometimes hear *was* in informal spoken English.
Note: The two clauses can usually be used in either order; for example:
I'd travel around the world if I had $1 million.

Relative clauses

See Unit 17.

(The main clauses are in *italics*. The relative clauses are in **bold**.)
A cheetah is an animal **that can run at 60 mph**.
A person **who treats sick animals** *is called a vet*.
Meow is a noise **cats make**.
The people **my brother works with** *are all crazy*.

Grammar glossary

Phonetic symbols

main verb adjective conjunction modal auxiliary adverb article pronoun main verb

Learn these useful words and you can understand more about the language you are studying.

determiner noun pronoun main verb preposition noun auxiliary verb

Agents are people or things that perform an action in a passive sentence.
> For example: *She was pardoned by **President Clinton** in 2001.*

Clauses are groups of words containing a verb.

main clause | subordinate clause

> For example: | I waited, | but he didn't come.

> Note: Subordinate clauses are usually introduced by conjunctions.

Combinations refer to words that frequently occur together.
> For example: *common sense   get along well   Happy birthday*

Dynamic meaning is a way of referring to verbs when they describe actions. Verbs with dynamic meanings can be used in both simple and continuous verb forms.
> For example: *People usually **talk** to one another on the plane.*
> *Some people **are talking** in the next room.*

Expressions are groups of words that belong together where the words and word order never or rarely change.
> For example: ***black and white**   That reminds me, I have to buy some toothpaste.*
> *How do you do?*

Idioms are expressions with a meaning that cannot be understood by knowing the meaning of each individual word.
> For example: *It's **a piece of cake**. = It's really easy.*
> *Don't **spill the beans**. = Don't tell the secret.*

***If*-clauses** are used to introduce conditions where we can describe a real situation (possible) or an unreal situation (improbable or impossible).
> For example: *If the weather is nice, we'll go on a picnic.* (real situation)
> *If I won the lottery, I'd quit my job and never work again.* (unreal situation)

Intransitive verbs do not take an object.
> For example: *He **walked**.   Is Marta still **sleeping**?   **Sit down**!*

Objects usually come after the verb and show who or what is affected by the verb.
> For example: *She closed **the window**.   My neighbor hates **me**.   I made **a pot of coffee**.*
> Note: Some verbs take a direct object (DO) and an indirect object (IO).

IO DO   IO DO   IO DO
> For example: *She gave* | him | a kiss |. *He sent* | her | some flowers |. *I teach* | students | English |.

Particles are adverbs or prepositions that form part of a phrasal verb.
> For example: *sit **down**   turn **off**   call **up***

Phrasal verbs are verbs consisting of a main verb + particle(s). Phrasal verbs are sometimes referred to as two- or three-word verbs.
> For example: ***grow up**   take your shoes **off**   I ran **after** the bus.*

Relative clauses give additional information about a <u>thing</u> or a <u>person</u> introduced in the main clause.
> For example: *A turtle is an <u>animal</u> **that can live to seventy years old**.*
> *The <u>people</u> **my brother works with** are all crazy.*

Relative pronouns such as *who, that,* and *which* are always used when they are the subject of the verb in a relative clause.

subject | verb | object
> For example: *People* | who | don't eat | meat | *are called vegetarians.*

subject | verb | object
> *I have a parrot* | that | can speak | English |.

Stative meaning is a way of referring to verbs when they describe states. Verbs with stative meanings cannot be used with continuous verb forms.
> For example: *I **want** a fairer system.* (NOT ~~I'm wanting a fairer system.~~)
> *I've **known** him for years.* (NOT ~~I've been knowing him for years.~~)

Subjects usually come before the verb and refer to the main person or thing you are talking about.
> For example: ***Money** doesn't grow on trees.   **My tailor** is rich.*
> ***The biggest rock group in the world** has started a world tour.*

VOWELS

/ɪ/	big fish	/bɪg fɪʃ/
/i/	green beans	/grin binz/
/ʊ/	should look	/ʃʊd lʊk/
/u/	blue moon	/blu mun/
/ɛ/	ten eggs	/tɛn ɛgz/
/ə/	about mother	/əbaʊt mʌðər/
/æ/	fat cat	/fæt kæt/
/ʌ/	must come	/mʌst kʌm/
/ɔ/	fall ball	/fɔl bɔl/
/ɑ/	hot spot	/hɑt spɑt/

DIPHTHONGS

/ei/	face	/feis/
/ɔi/	boy	/bɔi/
/ou/	nose	/nouz/
/ai/	eye	/ai/
/au/	mouth	/mauθ/

CONSONANTS

/p/	pen	/pɛn/
/b/	bad	/bæd/
/t/	tea	/ti/
/d/	dog	/dɔg/
/tʃ/	church	/tʃərtʃ/
/dʒ/	jazz	/dʒæz/
/k/	cost	/kɔst/
/g/	girl	/gərl/
/f/	far	/fɑr/
/v/	voice	/vɔis/
/θ/	thin	/θɪn/
/ð/	then	/ðɛn/
/s/	snake	/sneik/
/z/	noise	/nɔiz/
/ʃ/	shop	/ʃap/
/ʒ/	measure	/mɛʒər/
/m/	make	/meik/
/n/	nine	/nain/
/ŋ/	sing	/sɪŋ/
/h/	house	/haus/
/l/	leg	/lɛg/
/r/	red	/rɛd/
/w/	wet	/wɛt/
/y/	yes	/yɛs/

STRESS

In this book, word stress is shown by underlining the stressed syllable.
For example: <u>wa</u>ter; re<u>sult</u>; disa<u>ppoin</u>ting

LETTERS OF THE ALPHABET

/ei/	/i/	/ɛ/	/ai/	/ou/	/u/	/ɑr/
Aa	Bb	Ff	Ii	Oo	Qq	Rr
Hh	Cc	Ll	Yy		Uu	
Jj	Dd	Mm			Ww	
Kk	Ee	Nn				
	Gg	Ss				
	Pp	Xx				
	Tt					
	Vv					
	Zz					

Irregular verbs

Simple form	Simple past	Past participle
be	was/were	been
beat	beat	beaten
become	became	become
begin	began	begun
bend	bent	bent
bet	bet	bet
bite	bit	bitten
blow	blew	blown
break	broke	broken
bring	brought	brought
build	built	built
burn	burned	burned
burst	burst	burst
buy	bought	bought
can	could	(been able)
catch	caught	caught
choose	chose	chosen
come	came	come
cost	cost	cost
cut	cut	cut
deal	dealt	dealt
do	did	done
draw	drew	drawn
dream	dreamed	dreamed
drink	drank	drunk
drive	drove	driven
eat	ate	eaten
fall	fell	fallen
feed	fed	fed
feel	felt	felt
fight	fought	fought
find	found	found
fly	flew	flown
forget	forgot	forgotten
forgive	forgave	forgiven
freeze	froze	frozen
get	got	gotten
give	gave	given
go	went	gone
grow	grew	grown
hang	hung/hanged	hung/hanged
have	had	had
hear	heard	heard
hide	hid	hidden
hit	hit	hit
hold	held	held
hurt	hurt	hurt
keep	kept	kept
kneel	knelt/kneeled	knelt/kneeled
know	knew	known
lay	laid	laid
lead	led	led
learn	learned	learned
leave	left	left
lend	lent	lent
let	let	let

Simple form	Simple past	Past participle
lie	lay/lied	lain/lied
light	lit/lighted	lit/lighted
lose	lost	lost
make	made	made
mean	meant	meant
meet	met	met
must	had to	(had to)
pay	paid	paid
put	put	put
read	read /rɛd/	read /rɛd/
ride	rode	ridden
ring	rang	rung
rise	rose	risen
run	ran	run
say	said	said
see	saw	seen
sell	sold	sold
send	sent	sent
set	set	set
shake	shook	shaken
shine	shined/shone	shined/shone
shoot	shot	shot
show	showed	shown
shrink	shrank	shrunk
shut	shut	shut
sing	sang	sung
sink	sank	sunk
sit	sat	sat
sleep	slept	slept
slide	slid	slid
smell	smelled	smelled
speak	spoke	spoken
spell	spelled	spelled
spend	spent	spent
spill	spilled	spilled
split	split	split
spoil	spoiled	spoiled
spread	spread	spread
stand	stood	stood
steal	stole	stolen
stick	stuck	stuck
swear	swore	sworn
swell	swelled	swollen/swelled
swim	swam	swum
take	took	taken
teach	taught	taught
tear	tore	torn
tell	told	told
think	thought	thought
throw	threw	thrown
understand	understood	understood
wake	woke	woken
wear	wore	worn
win	won	won
write	wrote	written

Tapescripts

11 Smile

▭ **46**

(See page 64.)

▭ **47**

(See page 65.)

▭ **48**

(See page 65.)

▭ **49**

(See page 65.)

▭ **50**

a) I'd love to meet your friends—let's make a date now. We could try that new restaurant on 48th Street.

b) No, no, don't do it like that. Do it like this. Go on, do it again, and, oh, then get me some coffee.

c) No problem—I'm sure I can win. I know I'm faster than the others.

d) I'm working here to get some experience, but I'm going to start up my own company soon.

e) Yeah, whatever—I really don't mind. I'll be happy if we go out. I'll be happy if we stay in. Let's do whatever you want to do.

f) Look, are you sure you're O.K., because I can stay longer if you want. Anyway, you know where I am if you need me. Take care.

▭ **51**

(See page 67.)

▭ **52**

Laughter Clubs

Scientific research has proved that laughter reduces the effects of stress and helps the body to fight against illness and infection. In India, the health benefits of laughter are taken very seriously. There is a network of 600 "laughter clubs" where people meet every day just to laugh. They participate in "social laughter" (quiet tittering), suppressed laughter (snickering), and the loud, explosive laugh (roaring with laughter) that exercises the lungs.

12 Rebel

▭ **53**

(I = Interviewer; J = Jake; D = Debbie; R = Ronny; C = Caroline)

I: It's May 1, and we are in the middle of a huge May Day demonstration. People are handing out leaflets with information. There are all kinds of people here, but what exactly are they protesting about?

Jake

I: Excuse me! Yes, you. What are you doing here?

J: I'm protesting against globalization. Multinational companies cause a lot of pollution. They are polluting the world's rivers and oceans, and they don't care—they just want to make as much money as possible. I'm also giving out peaceful protest leaflets and T-shirts. There are some people here who want violence, but most people are here to protest in a peaceful way. Me, I'm a supporter of peaceful action.

I: Thank you.

Debbie

I: Excuse me. Can you tell me what you're doing here?

D: Well, I'm in favor of many of the causes here, but I'm here today with a group of women from Texas. We're demonstrating for equal pay for women. Women still earn less than men in most jobs, and it's time for that to change. I'm not anti-men—I just want a fairer system. Would you like to sign our petition?

I: Uh, yes, sure, thank you.

Ronny

I: Hi there! Can you tell me what you're doing here?

R: I'm selling veggieburgers. I'm against cosmetic companies that use animals in their experiments. At home I have three dogs, two cats, and a pet mouse named Jerry. They are my friends. I support animal rights, and I'm protesting against cruelty to animals. All right?

I: Good luck.

Caroline

I: Excuse me. What are you doing here?

C: I'm having fun with my friends. I don't feel strongly about politics, and I don't know much about it. This is my first demonstration. I'm really against the destruction of the rain forest. You know, the logging companies are destroying the forests. This is really serious. Each of us has to be responsible for protecting the natural environment. I really care about a clean, safe environment for our children. We owe it to them.

▭ **54**

(See page 71.)

▭ **55**

explain, explanation
organize, organization
produce, production
legalize, legalization
educate, education
reduce, reduction
modernize, modernization
legislate, legislation

▭ **56**

(See page 74.)

13 Dance

▭ **57**

(I = Interviewer; J = Josh; S = Simone; A = Antonio)

Josh

I: Josh, how are you?

J: Uh, to be honest, I'm really beat! I've been dancing all night.

I: Hey, how come you don't have a tan? Don't you like sunbathing?

J: Uh, well, I haven't been to the beach yet.

I: How come? How long have you been here?

J: Dunno. Nine, ten days.

I: Well, what have you been doing since you arrived?

J: I've been clubbing every night and sleeping all day. I've met loads of people, especially girls.

I: So, have you had a good time?

J: Oh yeah, definitely. I reckon this is the best vacation I've ever had. The only problem is I'm broke. I've spent all my money, and I still have a few days to go.

I: Yeah, well, good luck and have a good trip home.

J: Thanks. Say…you couldn't lend me some money, could you?

Simone

I: Simone, how long have you been here?

S: Since 1997.

I: Where are you from originally?

S: Brazil, but I haven't been home in a couple of years now.

I: What have you been doing here since 1997?

S: Having a great time—I've been working in clubs. I've been a resident DJ at Amnesia for two years. Oh, and I've been building my own house.

I: Really? Do you make a lot of money working in clubs?

S: You can, but I've also married a guy from Ibiza. His father gave us the land to build a house.

I: I see. Do you think you'll ever go back to Brazil?

S: Well, I love the lifestyle here; it's so laid back. And anyway, all my friends and family come and visit me here.

Antonio

I: Good morning, Antonio. How are you today?

A: Not bad, not bad. But I've been working all night in my restaurant, so I'm going to go to bed soon.

I: Well, thanks for talking to us. How long have you been here in Ibiza?

A: All my life. I was born in the north, but I've been living in Ibiza since 1995. That was when I opened my own restaurant.

I: What's it like living here in Ibiza?

A: Ah, it used to be a wonderful place, but now the tourists have ruined it.

I: But tourists have been coming to Ibiza since the sixties.

A: That's true, but they've changed. Tourists used to behave much better than they do today. They used to be polite and quiet. Now it's all noise and wild parties.

I: What types of people come to your restaurant?

A: Well…uh…tourists.

▭ 58

(See page 81.)

14 Call

▭ 59

(M = Mom; L = Lorna)

M: Hello.

L: Hi, Mom. It's me.

M: Oh, hello, darling. How are you?

L: I can't hear you, Mom. It's a really bad connection.

M: Sorry, dear. I said how are you?

L: Terrible, Mom. My back's killing me, and the house is a mess.

M: Don't worry, darling, I'll come and help you clean the house.

L: But that's not all—the kids are driving me crazy. ELLA, PUT HIM DOWN!

M: Don't worry, darling. After we've cleaned the house, I'll take the children to the park.

L: Oh thanks, Mom. There is something else though. ELLA, I SAID PUT HIM DOWN! Sorry—the thing is, I'm expecting six people for dinner, and there's nothing to eat. Do you think you could do some shopping on your way over here?

M: No problem, darling. I'll stop at the supermarket, and then I'll make a dinner your friends will never forget.

L: Thanks, Mom. I don't know what I'd do without you. Could you do one more thing for me?

M: Of course, darling, what is it?

L: Well, I've run out of money. Could you possibly pay for the shopping, and I'll pay you back at the end of the month?

M: That's fine. You don't have to pay me back.

▭ 60

(L = Lorna; M = Mom)

L: Mom—you're an angel. How's Dad?

M: Dad? Darling, you know your father and I divorced when you were thirteen.

L: Divorced? Thirteen? Oh no—what number is this?

M: 555-4450.

L: Oh, no! I don't believe it. I dialed the wrong number.

M: Juliet?

L: I'm not Juliet—but please, wait—does this mean you're not coming over?

▭ 61

Conversation 1

(D = Dad; L = Lorna)

D: Hello.

L: Dad?

D: Hello, dear. How are you?

L: Oh, not too good actually.

D: Oh, dear, what's the matter?

L: PUT THAT DOWN!

D: What?!

L: No, not, not you, Dad—the children are driving me crazy. NO! FREDDIE, WHY DID YOU DO THAT?

D: Look, dear, I'm just going out to play golf. Can I call you back later? Or should I leave a message for your mother to call you when she comes in?

L: Yes. Please. Could you tell her it's urgent?

D: Yes, O.K., dear—I think she'll be home…

L: FREDDIE—DON'T TOUCH THAT! Dad, I have to go.

D: Oh—goodbye, dear.

Conversation 2

(J = Jackie; L = Lorna)

J: Hello.

L: Hello. Is this Jackie?

J: Yes. Hold on a minute…(Turn the music down!)

L: Jackie, it's Lorna. Lorna Carr.

J: Oh, hello, Mrs. Carr.

L: I was wondering if you could come over and baby-sit for a couple of hours this afternoon.

J: This afternoon? Uh…Would you mind hanging on a minute, please?…(I have to go and babysit.)…Is it O.K. if I bring my boyfriend?

L: Yes, that's fine. Would you like me to drive over and pick you up?

J: It's O.K. We'll take the bus.

L: NO! Uh, no, I need you right now. I'll be right over.

▭ 62

(See page 85.)

…and here are some useful phone numbers for tourists in the New York area. Remember — if you call on a cell phone, you do not have to dial the first one. And here are the numbers.

For trains to anywhere in the United States, call Amtrak for train schedules and fare information at one eight hundred…eight seven two…seven two four five.

For car rentals, call Budget Rent-A-Car. The number is one seven one eight…six five six…six oh one oh.

If you have problems with your car, call the Triple A emergency road service number at one eight hundred…two two two…four three five seven.

If you want to go by bus from New York City to anywhere, call the Port Authority Bus Terminal at one two one two…five oh two…two three four one.

For information about trains from New York to New Jersey, call PATH train information at one eight hundred…two three four…seven six two four.

And remember, if you need a phone number anywhere in the United States, call four one one for Directory Assistance.

64

A
A: Dad…Do you think I could have a Zoomatron for my birthday?… Please?
B: What's a Zoomatron?
A: It's a kind of space gun. It's really cool.
B: Oh, no. Not another one…
A: Please.

B
A: Could you tell me where the restroom is?
B: What?
A: Do you know where the restrooms are?
B: Sorry—I can't hear you.
A: WHERE'S THE RESTROOM?
B: Over there.

C
A: Can you remember where we left it?
B: Uhm, I think it was on the second level.

A: Well, this is the second level, and I can't see it.
B: I think we parked next to a white van.…There it is.

D
A: Do you have any idea what the time is?
B: Dunno.
A: Well, it's twelve thirty. Where on earth have you been? I've been worried sick. Wait till your father hears about this!

E
A: Do you know if the last bus has left?
B: I'm afraid it left a couple of minutes ago.
A: Oh, no! Do you know where I can get a taxi?
B: Try the train station—there are usually a few taxis there.
A: Thanks.

F
A: Excuse me—do you know where the lions are?
B: They're over there next to the giraffes.
A: O.K. Thank you.

15 Review 3

65

(R = Reporter; H = Hyacinth; D = Derek; M = Maria; O = Oona; S = Sara)

Interview 1
R: Excuse me, ma'am, would you mind answering a few questions for 1010 Radio Sports News?
H: Certainly.
R: Well, could you tell me where you come from? Have you come far?
H: We don't live far from here. We live in Richmond, actually, so we usually get here very early in the morning. We like to be at the front of the queue, but Derek was slow getting up this morning, and there was a bit of a problem on the Underground, so we arrived a little later than usual.
R: Could you tell me how long you've been waiting?
H: Since about half past eight, something like that, I suppose. So, yes, it's been a long wait. What is it—about three o'clock now? Derek! What's the time now? Derek!
D: Yes, dear?

R: Do you think you'll get in?
H: Oh yes, I think we'll probably get in soon. Won't we, Derek? Derek, stop looking at that girl! You've been looking at her for hours. Haven't you seen enough? She's certainly not interested in you!
R: Well, it's a long queue. Do you know how many people there are in front of you?
H: I imagine there are about, what, twenty or thirty people. It won't be long now, will it, Derek?
D: Huh?

Interview 2
R: Excuse me, would you mind answering a few questions for 1010 Radio Sports News?
M: Excuse me? Can you speak a little more slowly, please?
R: Sure. Can I ask you a few questions for the radio?
M: Yes, of course.
R: How long have you been waiting here?
M: I have been waiting here since eight fifteen this morning. I did not know there was a long line.
R: You must be a real tennis fan!
M: Ah, so-so. I am a student of English. I have been in London for four weeks, and tomorrow I have to go back to Bogotá in Colombia, and I thought it was a good idea to come to Wimbledon before I go back to Colombia.
R: Do you think you'll get in?
M: Excuse me?
R: Do you think you will get in?
M: No, I do not think so. It has been raining since one thirty. I am wet and cold, and I am hungry, and there are many, many people in front of me in line. I think I will give up soon.

Interview 3
R: Excuse me, ma'am, would you mind answering a few questions for 1010 Radio Sports News?
O: Oh, come under the umbrella, dear. Would you like a strawberry?
R: Mm, thanks. Have you been here long?
O: Ooh, I'm not sure. What time did we arrive, Sara?
S: Mm, about eight?
O: Yes, we've been here since about eight this morning. We come every year on the Friday, you know.
R: What are your chances of getting in?

O: Not very good, I would say. It rained on the Friday last year, too, and we never got in. But you never know. There are probably about fifty people in front of us, but lots of them will give up and go home soon. Maybe we'll get the last match of the day. We live in Scotland, you know, so this is a big day out for us. We're not giving up now, not after coming all this way.

R: Isn't it a long time to wait for one match?

O: Ooh, no. We love the tennis, of course, but we really come for the atmosphere. We've met so many interesting people since we arrived. Have you spoken to that charming young girl from Colombia? We've been chatting for ages—she speaks English really well. And Sara always brings her radio, so we've been listening to that. We've been having a great day, haven't we, Sara?

S: Mm, another strawberry?

R: Mm, thanks. Well, good luck with the wait!

📼 66

(See page 90.)

📼 67

(S = Secretary; MK = Mrs. Knightly)

S: Mr. Rogers' office. Can I help you?

MK: Oh, hello. Can I speak to Mr. Rogers, please?

S: Certainly. Could you hold for a minute, please? I'm sorry, but Mr. Rogers is not in yet, ma'am.

MK: Uh, would you mind taking a message?

S: Certainly.

MK: Uhm, well, it's Joanna Knightly. I have an appointment with Mr. Rogers at 9:15, and I'm sorry, but I missed the bus…

S: Would you like to give me your telephone number, and I'll ask Mr. Rogers to call you when he gets in?

MK: That's all right, thanks. I'll call back later.

S: You're welcome. Goodbye.

MK: Thanks. Goodbye.

📼 68

(See page 93.)

16 Lifestyle

📼 69

(R = Receptionist; W = Woman)

R: New Life Center. Can I help you?

W: Yes. Could you give me some information about your center?

R: Certainly. Are you interested in losing weight or just improving your fitness?

W: Uhm, it's not for me. It's for my husband. He needs to lose weight and improve his fitness. I want to give him a week at your center as a surprise for his birthday.

R: Ah, lucky man!

W: Could you tell me something about the program?

R: Sure. As soon as he arrives here, he'll take a fitness test to see what kind of diet he needs to go on.

W: I see.

R: We start every day at 7:30 with a half-hour walk before breakfast.

W: Ha ha. He usually starts the day with a cigarette before breakfast!

R: I don't think so. If he has a cigarette here, he'll be in big trouble. It's a strictly no-smoking area.

W: Well, it's a good idea for him to give up smoking. He says he'll give it up as soon as he feels more relaxed.

R: Well, this is the ideal place to relax. We do at least two hours of yoga and meditation every day, and after the morning hike, he can have a sauna and jacuzzi.

W: Oh, he'll enjoy that. But what's this hike?

R: They go for a hike in the morning from 8:30 to 12:30. One of our instructors will take your husband and other people at the same level of fitness for a four-hour hike into the mountains.

W: Four hours! His idea of a walk is going from the front door to his car.

R: Oh, don't worry. When they get to the top of the mountain, they'll have a twenty-minute break before they come down again. The scenery is very relaxing.

W: They'll be starving!

R: Oh, don't worry. When they're hungry, they'll stop for a healthy snack. The instructor always carries a supply of fruit.

W: So no chocolate? Hmm. And what about the afternoon? Can he relax then?

R: No, not really. But he'll have time to relax after the afternoon hike.

W: Oh my goodness. I don't think he'll thank me for this.

R: Believe me, when he finishes the week, he'll feel like a new man.

W: If he finishes the week!

📼 70

(See page 98.)

📼 71

/ɪ/ lettuce   spinach
/ʌ/ onion   nut
/ə/ banana   lemon
/i/ sardines   beans
/ɑ/ orange   olive
/ou/ potato   tomato

📼 72

(See page 98.)

17 Animals

📼 73

1 Word A: tail – T A I L tail.
  Word B: tale – T A L E tale.
2 Word A: deer – D E E R deer.
  Word B: dear – D E A R dear.
3 Word A: bear – B E A R bear.
  Word B: bare – B A R E bare.
4 Word A: right – R I G H T right.
  Word B: write – W R I T E write.
5 Word A: wait – W A I T wait.
  Word B: weight – W E I G H T weight.

📼 74

(See page 103.)

📼 75

a) Tim

(I = Interviewer; T = Tim)

I: Can you describe your pet?

T: She's very fat and not very pretty. But she has a beautiful curly tail.

I: What does she eat?

T: Anything and everything. She's very fond of banana skins.

I: Is she a good companion?

T: Yes, I always go and talk to her when I'm in a bad mood. She listens to my problems when no one else will.

I: When you go away, who takes care of her?

T: If I go away for work, my girlfriend looks after her. But if my girlfriend goes on the trip with me, we have to take her over to my parents. She doesn't like that very much because they have a dog that annoys her.

I: Do you and your pet look alike?

T: I hope not.

I: If you were an animal, what animal would you like to be?

T: I used to say a dolphin when I was younger, but I don't like the ocean very much now. I don't know—a giraffe maybe, though I'd hate to be stuck in a zoo.

b) Gus

(I = Interviewer; G = Gus)

I: Can you describe your pet?

G: He's black and has eight hairy legs.

I: What does he eat?

G: Insects.

I: What, he catches them?

G: No, I buy them frozen.

I: Is he a good companion?

G: Yeah. He's like a friend. We have a special bond.

I: When you go away, who takes care of him?

G: Well, I haven't been away since I got him, and I don't think anybody wants to take care of him. Certainly not my mom. He scares people away.

I: Do you and your pet look alike?

G: I'm not that hairy—but I think he looks cool, like me.

I: If you were an animal, what animal would you like to be?

G: A lion, because they're big and tough, and they rule.

c) Maxine

(I = Interviewer; M = Maxine)

I: Can you describe your pet?

M: She's very fluffy and very lovable. My boyfriend doesn't like her because she bit him—she's definitely a girl's girl.

I: What does she eat?

M: Her favorite foods are fresh vegetables, nuts, and cereal.

I: Is she a good companion?

M: Oh, yes, I love Page because she's good company for me when my boyfriend is away traveling. Besides, we have the same interests—she loves to sleep all day, eat, and then she parties all night long.

I: When you go away, who takes care of her?

M: I take her everywhere in her little cage.

I: Do you and your pet look alike?

M: I think that she's better looking than me—who could resist those brown button eyes?

I: If you were an animal, what animal would you like to be?

M: I am an animal.

🔊 76

I know somebody who has an iguana as a pet. It's a man I work with named Harry. The iguana is named Iggy, and it's probably about five years old—that's how long I've known Harry, and he got it soon after we met. It was a birthday present from his wife. It's just over three feet long from the tip of its nose to the end of its tail, and it's a lovely green color. Like all reptiles, iguanas never stop growing, so Iggy will get bigger and bigger. It's kind of shy and nervous, which is exactly the opposite of Harry, who's very outgoing and confident. It's definitely better looking than Harry though. Iggy doesn't sleep in a cage. For now, it lives at the top of the curtains in Harry's living room. When it was young, it ate crickets, but now that it's an adult, it doesn't need so much protein—in fact, it's completely vegetarian. Harry takes it for walks in the park on a leash. It's funny—when it's frightened, it runs up Harry's body and sits on his head.

18 Weird

🔊 77

(A = Anchorperson; I = Ida Gomez; K = Ken Crystal)

A: Let's hear now from our correspondent, Ida Gomez, in our studios in England with a strange and mysterious story. Ida?

I: This morning the residents of a small village in Wiltshire woke up to an amazing sight. It is the biggest crop circle ever seen in Britain. The press is calling it the mother of all circles, and the question everyone is asking: How did it get there? In the studio with me today is Ken Crystal, a crop circle expert. Ken, how long have you been interested in crop circles?

K: For about eleven years now.

I: Can you tell us something about this circle?

K: Well, we're very excited about this crop circle. The design is absolutely amazing, and it's enormous.

I: How big is it exactly?

K: It's about a half a mile! We've never seen anything like this before!

I: It's a very complex design. How many circles are there all together?

K: There are more than 400 circles—it really is incredible.

I: And do you know who made it?

K: No, I don't, but I believe that this is the work of strange forces.

I: What do you mean?

K: It's impossible for people to make something like this.

I: But I've heard that most circles are made by people. Is that true?

K: Yes, there are several groups of people who make crop circles. But they didn't make this one.

I: How do you know?

K: This circle appeared yesterday morning. The day before that, it wasn't there. There were only four hours of darkness that night—there wasn't enough time to make it.

I: How long does it take to make a crop circle?

K: Well, a simple circle takes a few hours. But a circle like this one would take several days.

I: How long have crop circles existed?

K: The first crop circles were reported in 1980. In the last eleven years, I've visited over a thousand. But I've never seen one like this.

I: Ken, a final question. Do you think that this crop circle is the work of aliens?

K: I think it could be a message…

🔊 78
(See page 108.)

🔊 79
(See page 109.)

🔊 80
(See page 110.)

81

1 Don's Story

I had a strange experience while I was working in Massachusetts.

One Friday, I left Boston and went to Cape Cod for the weekend. I remember I was walking down a road—I was alone, and I was wearing a coat with a hood over my head because it was snowing.

Suddenly I heard somebody call my name. When I looked around, I saw that it was a young woman I'd met the previous summer in San Francisco. I live in San Francisco, and she had been on vacation there. After the vacation, she'd returned to Boston, her hometown, and I hadn't been in touch with her since then.

She had no idea that I was in Massachusetts, and she didn't even live in Cape Cod—she was just visiting a friend. But somehow she recognized me, even though it was snowing and I was wearing a big hood.

After that we stayed in touch, and in fact, she came to my wedding ten years later.

2 Lidia's Story

My sister and my aunt had a strange experience the day after my mother died.

At the time of her death, my mother was living with my sister. My aunt came to stay with my sister to help her make arrangements for the funeral.

In the afternoon, the two women were sitting in the living room when my sister's little dog started barking.

They went out of the room to see why the dog was barking, and they both saw my mother's shadow on the wall. The shadow came down the stairs and disappeared.

They said they weren't frightened, but of course, they felt very emotional.

Actually, my mother's ghost often appears to different members of the family, in different forms.

I think this is because she was such a strong character, and her memory lives on in our minds.

19 Wheels

82

(K = Karen; R = Ron; J = Jill)

K: You're late!

R: Yes, I'm really sorry—I had to wait forever for a bus.

J: Why didn't you drive?

R: Ah, well. I sold my car.

K: Oh, are you getting a new one?

R: No, I'm not getting another car. I've decided to live without one.

J: Wow—what made you do that?

R: I think there are too many cars, and this city is far too polluted.

J: Well, that's true, but a car is useful.

R: I don't think so. Not in the city, anyway. I can never find anywhere to park, and you spend most of the time sitting in traffic jams.

K: But how are you going to get to work?

R: By bicycle.

K: Don't you think bicycles are dangerous?

R: Not really. I don't think they're as dangerous as cars.

J: Well, I couldn't do without my car. I have to take the kids to school every day.

R: I don't think children get enough exercise these days—they should walk to school.

K: Well, I don't have children, but I agree with Jill—I couldn't live without my car. I sometimes have to come home late from the office.

R: Why don't you take the bus? Public transportation is very good.

K: That's not true. The buses are not very regular where I work, and anyway, as a woman, I don't feel safe waiting for a bus late at night.

R: O.K., I see what you mean, but aren't you worried about pollution?

J: Of course, but you don't understand—it's easy for you to worry about the environment. I have to worry about carrying the groceries and kids and…

R: O.K., O.K., you're right! Come on. Let's change the subject. Hey, what do you think of my new haircut?

83

(See page 114.)

84

(P = Dave Pearl, talk show host; C1 = Caller 1; C2 = Caller 2)

P: Welcome to the show. My name's Dave Pearl, and you're listening to *Road Rage*. O.K., let's see who's on the line. Hello—what's your name, and how can we help?

C1: Hello, Dave. Uh, my name's Mark, and my problem is traffic jams. I waste too much time sitting in my car in traffic jams in the morning on my way to work and on my way home after work, and I'm sick of it.

P: Ah, yes. I'm sure lots of people share your feelings, Mark. Why don't you work at home some of the time?

C1: I can't do that, Dave—I work in a store.

P: Oh, O.K. You could use public transportation. Then you could read a newspaper on your way to work, and your time wouldn't be wasted.

C1: I can't do that, Dave—I have to use my car at work for deliveries.

P: O.K. Well, Mark, if I were you, I'd learn a new language! Where do you want go on your next vacation?

C1: Uh, Mexico, Dave.

P: Great! You can buy a Spanish language course on CDs and play them on your car stereo. They're fantastic, and the time will pass quickly.

C1: Uh, Dave…

P: Thank you, Mark. Do we have another caller on the line—yes, hello—what's your name, and how can we help?

C2: Uh, hello, Dave. My name's…I'm, I'm Sharon, and I can't pass my driver's test.

P: Really? Why not?

C2: Well, I'm too nervous.

P: I see. How many times have you taken your test?

C2: Seven times, Dave. I'm fine when I'm practicing my driving, but then on the day of the test, I fall apart. I start shaking, and I can't see the road.

P: Well, Sharon,…

85

(See page 116.)

86

(See page 117.)

B136 TAPESCRIPTS

20 Review 4

⏺ 87

(H = Host; A = Amy; J = Jack;
V = Vera)

H: Hi, and welcome to *Speak Up!*, the radio talk show where *you* get the chance to say what *you* think about the stories in the news today. ... In the news today is lottery winner Eva Alvarado. Yes, listeners, Eva Alvarado won $198 million, but she says she doesn't want to change her life. She loves her job in a children's home, and she wants to stay the way she is. Call us now at 212 555-8989 and tell us what *you* think. ... We have our first caller—Amy Wilder. Go ahead, Amy.

A: Well, Mrs. Alvarado is obviously very fond of the children, but I'm sure she'll quit her job soon. When everybody knows how rich she is, life will be very difficult. Everyone will ask her for money, and she will soon get tired of all the letters. So she needs to think about the future now.

H: Good point there. We have Jack Nichols on the line. Go ahead, Jack.

J: Well, she doesn't sound very excited about winning the lottery. In fact, she's more interested in the children than in the money, so she'll probably give most of the money away—to the children's home, to her friends, you know? And I think she's right. If you have that much money, how are you going to spend it all?

H: Well, Jack, I'm sure I could help her! O.K., let's go to our next caller—Vera Baker.

V: It's a lot of money, and she'll need a financial advisor. She doesn't have to worry about the future anymore, but as soon as she has had time to think about it, I'm pretty sure she'll change her mind about just giving money to the children's home.

⏺ 88

(See page 121.)